CUBE
BOOK

GARDENS

WHITE STAR PUBLISHERS

EDITED BY

VALERIA MANFERTO DE FABIANIS

text by
OVIDIO GUAITA

editorial coordination
GIADA FRANCIA

graphic design
CLARA ZANOTTI

graphic layout
MARIA CUCCHI

text translation
CATHERINE BOLTON

captions translation
MADDALENA NEALE
KARLA DONNELLY
GLENN DEBATTISTA

© 2008 WHITE STAR S.P.A.
VIA CANDIDO SASSONE, 22-24
13100 VERCELLI – ITALY
WWW.WHITESTAR.IT

● A garden of the Alhambra, in Granada, Spain.

ISBN 978-88-544-0375-8
REPRINTS:
1 2 3 4 5 6   12   11 10 09 08
Printed in Singapore

CONTENTS

GARDENS

1 • Sculpted hedges in the Topiary Garden at Leven's Hall, in Cumbria, U.K.

2-3 • A blooming parterre in front of the royal palace of Versailles.

4-5 • A detail of the Grand Cascade in the garden of the Peterhof Palace near St Petersburg.

6-7 • An interior courtyard of the Lake Palace Hotel in Udaipur, in Rajasthan, India.

8-9 • A Japanese garden painted in autumn colors.

13 • Fantasy and reality intermingle in this zoomorphic composition.

14-15 • A gardener at work at the Château of Vaux-le-Vicomte, France.

16-17 • Two sculpted figures embrace in a garden of the Peterhof Palace, near St Petersburg.

Introduction

IN THE BEGINNING GOD CREATED A GARDEN, A PLACE OF PEACE AND PLEASURE, ABUNDANCE AND SERENITY: PARADISE ON EARTH. EDEN CONVEYS MAN'S NOSTALGIA FOR PERFECT NATURE AND REVEALS THE HUMAN ASPIRATION FOR A PLACE OF PEACE, WELL-BEING, BEAUTY AND PLENTY. SINCE THE FALL OF ADAM AND EVE HUMANITY HAS TRIED TO RECREATE THIS COSMOS, WHICH HAS COME TO SYMBOLIZE OUR FINAL DESTINATION, OUR REWARD IN THE AFTERLIFE. PERHAPS IT IS THIS DIVINE ORIGIN THAT HAS MADE GARDENS SO IMPORTANT IN HUMAN HISTORY. OR PERHAPS IT IS THE PLEASURE OF STROLLING ALONG THE REDOLENT AVENUES THAT COMPOSE IT. EVEN WITHOUT STREAMS FLOWING WITH MILK, HONEY AND OTHER DELIGHTS CONTEMPLATED IN THE ISLAMIC PARADISE, THE GARDEN IS STILL CONSIDERED A BLISSFUL PLACE.

● The Temple of Love with a sculpture by Bourchardon, in a corner of the gardens at Versailles.

Introduction

THANKS TO THE GREEKS AND ROMANS, THE GARDEN BECAME A PATCH OF NATURE ORGANIZED ACCORDING TO HUMAN NEEDS: A PLACE TO GROW PLANTS, NOT ONLY TO PROVIDE NOURISHMENT BUT ALSO FOR THEIR BEAUTY. THE GARDENS OF IMPERIAL ROME REPRESENT ONE OF THE FIRST EXAMPLES OF ARCHITECTURAL GARDENS, IN WHICH GEOMETRIC ORGANIZATION WAS INSPIRED BY THE SYMMETRY OF VILLAS. ALTHOUGH THE REDISCOVERY OF GARDENS DURING THE MIDDLE AGES WAS ESSENTIALLY THE WORK OF THE CLERGY, SUBSEQUENT DEVELOPMENT WAS CHIEFLY SECULAR, AS CLEARLY REVEALED BY CHARLEMAGNE'S *CAPITULARE DE VILLIS VEL DE CURTIS IMPERATORIS*, A COLLECTION OF REGULATIONS ON THE CONSTRUCTION AND MAINTENANCE OF IMPERIAL PROPERTY. THE FAME OF THESE GARDENS SPREAD THROUGHOUT ITALY, BUT TUSCANY WAS THE ONLY ENVIRONMENT READY TO EMBRACE THIS NEW TREND. THE

Introduction

GARDEN OF THE FLORENTINE HUMANISTS OF THE EARLY 15TH CENTURY WAS AN EVOLVING GEOMETRIC SPACE THAT, IN SOME CASES, WAS STILL ENCLOSED. IN THE 16TH CENTURY, THE MOORISH GARDENS OF ANDALUSIA SERVED AS FORMAL AND TECHNOLOGICAL BENCHMARKS FOR WATER EFFECTS, BUT THE COURTS OF EUROPE ADOPTED THE ITALIAN STYLE OF CREATING GARDENS, TURNING TO RENAISSANCE AND FLORENTINE MODELS FOR INSPIRATION. THE RENAISSANCE GARDEN WAS A PLACE OF QUIET CONTEMPLATION, WHEREAS THE BAROQUE GARDEN BECAME THE LAVISH BACKDROP FOR CEREMONIES AND FESTIVITIES. BEFORE IT TOOK A ROMANTIC TURN, THE FORMAL GARDEN EXPANDED TO THE SCALE ADVOCATED BY FRENCH ARCHITECTS. WHEREAS THE ITALIAN GARDEN WAS BASED ON THE RELATIONSHIP BETWEEN MAN AND NATURE, VIEWING MAN AS PART OF THE UNIVERSE REPRESENTED BY THE LANDSCAPE, THE FRENCH

Introduction

GARDEN EXPRESSED THE HUMAN DESIRE TO DOMINATE NA-
TURE. IN ENGLAND, NATURE WAS INSTEAD REDISCOVERED
AND APPRECIATED IN ALL ITS UNPREDICTABILITY, AND WAS
"ASSISTED" WHEN IT DID NOT LOOK NATURAL ENOUGH.
TODAY'S GARDEN IS ALL THIS – AND JUST THE OPPOSITE. RE-
VIVALS AND REMAKES CREATE A DIZZYING ARRAY OF
TRENDS, IN WHICH THE SOLE LEITMOTIF IS THE PASSION FOR
DESIGNING GREENERY.

FLORAL PARADISES

- These boxwood forms appear among vibrant flowers in the parterre at the Château of Villandry, in the Loire Valley, France.

INTRODUCTION Floral Paradises

As is often the case with manmade works, genius can transform a simple project into a masterpiece. In terms of gardens, this consideration applies to most of the private parks established over the centuries in Europe and Asia, and – more recently – in the New World. Across the globe, the hand of man has produced masterpieces that, in their attempt to imitate or even improve nature, are rightly considered "corners of paradise" that have fallen to earth. Although the creation of gardens to adorn mansions is a modern concept, the oldest civilizations also produced breathtaking works. In America the only known native gardens are the Aztec *chinampas*, which amazed the Spanish conquerors. In the rest of the New World, the concept of the garden is a combination of local varieties and the fashions and trends im-

INTRODUCTION Floral Paradises

PORTED FROM EUROPE. IT IS A MELTING POT OF FORMS AND AL-
LUSIONS. IN NORTH AMERICA, THE PLANTATIONS OF VIRGINIA AND
LOUISIANA ARE THE BEST-KNOWN COLONIAL VERSIONS. IT WAS
NOT UNTIL THE 19TH AND 20TH CENTURIES THAT RESORT HOMES
BECAME POPULAR IN NEWPORT, LONG ISLAND AND PALM BEACH,
BRINGING WITH THEM ALL KINDS OF REVIVALS – INCLUDING GAR-
DENS. IN 15TH-CENTURY EUROPE THE HISTORY OF WESTERN GAR-
DENS WAS REVIVED AFTER THE HIATUS OF THE MIDDLE AGES. DU-
RING THIS PERIOD FLORENTINE HUMANISTS REDISCOVERED THE
CLASSICAL EXPERIENCES OF IMPERIAL ROME, AND THE ARABS
SETTLED IN ANDALUSIA, WHERE THEY SPREAD THEIR KNOWLEDGE
OF WATERWORKS. THE MIGRATION OF ARTISTS AND ARCHITECTS
HELPED SPREAD THE CONCEPT OF GARDENS VIRTUALLY
EVERYWHERE. SINCE THE 16TH CENTURY EUROPEAN EXPERIEN-
CES HAVE SET THE STANDARD AROUND THE WORLD, THE ONLY

Floral Paradises
Introduction

EXCEPTIONS BEING THE NEAR EAST AND COUNTRIES UNDER CHINESE AND JAPANESE INFLUENCE, WHICH DEVELOPED THEIR OWN TRADITION. THE LAND OF MANY ANCIENT CIVILIZATIONS, ASIA IS ALSO THE HOMELAND OF GARDENS, THE ORIGIN OF THE CONCEPT OF A GREEN SPACE CREATED FOR THE PLEASURES OF EARTHLY LIFE BUT MADE IN THE IMAGE OF THE AFTERLIFE: PARADISE ON EARTH. ALTHOUGH GARDENS WERE FIRST CREATED IN THE NEAR EAST AND THEIR FIRST AND BEST-KNOWN MANIFESTATIONS WERE THOSE OF BABYLON, THEY ALSO DEVELOPED IN MANY OTHER AREAS OF THE ASIAN CONTINENT. IN SOME CASES, THEY EVOLVED INDEPENDENTLY AND IN VERY DIFFERENT FORMS, SUCH AS THOSE OF KASHMIR, CHINA AND JAPAN, AND THE GARDEN CONCEPT IS ENTWINED WITH BOTH PHILOSOPHY AND RELIGION.

● The magnificence of the gardens of Peterhof Palace, near St Petersburg, Russia, is evident in this striking view.

38 ● A view of the fantastic scenery in the gardens of Isola Bella on Lake Maggiore, Italy.

39 ● A beautiful view looking out onto Lake Maggiore from the terraces of the gardens of Isola Bella.

40-41 • A terrace on the water of the Borromean island Isola Bella, with Lake Maggiore in the background.

41 • The Ninfeo on Isola Bella, the island on which Borromeo erected his 17th Century residence.

● A parterre on Isola Bella at Stresa, on Lake Maggiore, which enjoys a splendid view of the lake and its shores.

44-45 • A pool surrounded by blooming parterres in the garden of Villa Taranto on Lake Maggiore.

45 • Diverse shades of green embellish a parterre in the formal garden of Villa Taranto, on Lake Maggiore.

• The Baroque garden of the Villa D'Este in Tivoli, Italy, is a succession of fountains, pools, *ninfeos*, and spouts.

48-49 ● At the Villa Garzoni in Collodi, Tuscany the garden ascends, in a series of terraces, from the large parterre opposite the residence.

49 ● Two swans swim in a pool in the garden of Villa Garzoni in Collodi, Italy.

A solitary statue observes visitors to the garden at Villa Barbarigo in the Euganean Hills in the Veneto, Italy.

52-53 • An aerial view of the grandiose Royal Palace at Caserta, jewel of the Campanian Baroque style.

53 • The Baroque garden of the Royal Palace at Caserta contains a series of pools several miles long.

● The long, narrow garden of the Caserta Palace descends a hill towards the royal residence, in a series of pools and fountains.

The garden of Bomarzo in the province of Viterbo, Italy, is one of the most unique gardens ever constructed. Built by Prince Orsini, this garden holds the Park of Monsters, also called the Sacred Wood, which brings to life the fantasies of the nobleman.

58 • An elephant sculpted from volcanic rock on a hill at Bomarzo, in the Sacred Wood, province of Viterbo.

59 • The Hanging House is one of the curiosities that can be visited in the Park of Monsters, also known as the Sacred Wood, in Bomarzo.

60-61 • The Royal Palace of Versailles and its magnificently landscaped gardens served as inspiration for important Baroque works.

62-63 • The elaborate design of a parterre in the Baroque Garden of the Palace of Versailles.

64-65 • The Château of Chenonceau with its bridge form is one of the most distinctive of the Loire Valley in France.

The Garden of the Château of Villandry in the Loire Valley, France, is immense.

68 • A unique part of the garden at Villandry is the section dedicated to edible plants, where cabbages and other vegetables are visible.

69 • The Garden of Villandry photographed from above.

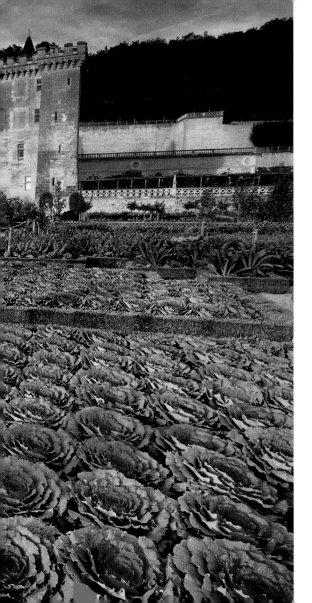

- In the Garden of Villandry in the Loire Valley, France, there is a very large section dedicated to vegetables.

72 ● A parterre with spirals and colorful
stones, in the Garden of the Château of
Vaux-le-Vicomte, near Paris, France.

72-73 ● Vaux-le-Vicomte is one of the
most striking French Baroque creations
after Versailles, not only for its large size
but also for its form.

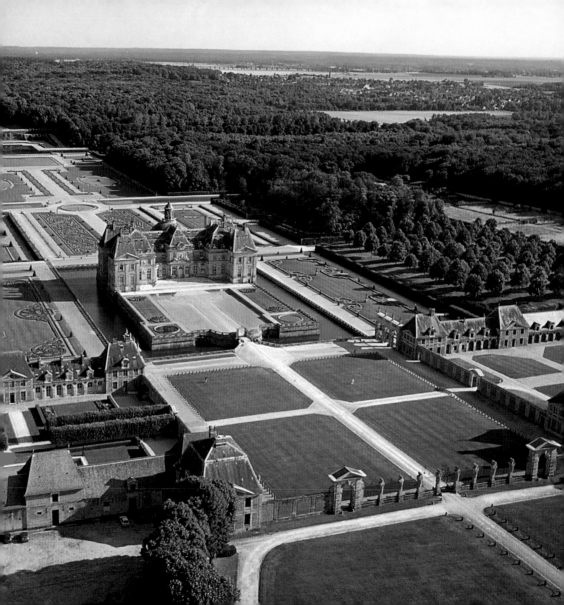

The summer residence of Sans Souci Palace at Potsdam near Berlin, Germany, has numerous secondary buildings.

76-77 ● The magnificent
orangery of Sans Souci Palace
in Potsdam, Germany, is reached
by a series of stairways.

77 ● Behind Sans Souci Palace
in Potsdam, near Berlin, Germany,
is a series of terraces with
greenhouses that hold potted
citrus trees.

78 • A view of the Palace and
the magnificent blooming
parterres of Schönbrunn,
in Vienna, Austria.

78-79 • Striking spirals drawn with
colorful flowers characterize the
Gardens of Schönbrunn Palace.

80 • The façade facing the gardens of Blenheim Palace in Oxfordshire, U.K.

81 • The embroidered parterre of boxwood spirals in front of Blenheim Palace in Oxfordshire, U.K.

The name of the residence, Blenheim Palace, is written in the circle at the center of this parterre located in Oxfordshire, U.K.

86-87 • Various topiary elements alternate with vases and pools in the gardens of the Royal Palace of Drottningholm at Stockholm, Sweden.

Rosenborg Castle stands, encircled by gardens, at the center of an island near Copenhagen, Denmark.

90-91 • Yellow and red roses predominate in the gardens of Powerscourt House, in Ireland.

91 • Sugarloaf Mountain is the background for the gardens of Powerscourt House, in Ireland.

92-93 • A pool in the garden of the Royal Palace of Queluz, located a few miles from Lisbon, Portugal.

94 • The sculptures of the Catholic Monarchs distinguish Alcatraz Garden in Cordoba, Andalusia, Spain.

95 • At the center of Alcatraz Garden in Cordoba, Spain, one can admire the beautiful pools.

96 • The formal garden created during the Renaissance within the Alcazar Palace in Seville, Spain.

97 • Pools bordered with geometric boxwoods are found in the gardens of the Alcazar Palace in Seville, Spain.

98 • The Court of the Long Pond in the garden of the Generalife in the Royal Palace of the Alhambra, which was built by the Arabs, in Granada, Spain.

99 • An Arab fountain with a spout in the courtyard of the Generalife at the Alhambra in Granada, Spain.

100-101 • The Partal is one of the oldest buildings of the Alhambra. The gardens surrounding it date to the 20th century.

102 ○ The Pazo de Oca Garden in Galicia, Spain, abounds in fountains and pools such as these.

103 ○ This ring of boxwood with half-spheres is part of the Pazo de Oca Garden in Galicia, Spain.

A view of the formal section of the gardens of the Royal Palace in Queluz, Portugal.

Tourists walk along
a path in Butchard
Gardens in Victoria,
British Columbia,
Canada.

108 • This section of the Filoli Garden in California, U.S.A., was created in the first decades of the 20th Century.

108-109 • This metal sundial on a pedestal is located at the intersection of two brick walkways in Filoli Garden in California, U.S.A.

110-111 • A Neoclassical clock tower dominates this area with a pool at the center of Filoli Garden in California, U.S.A.

111 • An expanse of flowers embellishes the informal section of the Filoli Garden in the U.S.A.

The autumn colors turn this
English-style park, located
on Long Island, in the U.S.A.,
into an enormous palette.

In 1974, Paul Getty had a reproduction of the Villa of Mysteries in Pompei built in Malibu, near Los Angeles, in the U.S.A.

116 and 117 • An expanse of succulents characterizes the Cactus Garden, located in the most recent section of the Paul Getty Museum in Malibu, California, U.S.A.

118-119 • The unmistakable cobalt blue is one of the distinguishing features of the buildings in the Majorelle Garden in Marrakech, Morocco.

120 • A few jacaranda trees create the backdrop for a clearing in the center of this informal garden, located on the Brenthurst Estate in South Africa.

121 • This path paved with rocks and stones in Brenthurst Garden ends in a curved bridge.

The wooden arch covered with violet wisteria frames the façade of the house on the Brenthurst Estate, in South Africa.

The sea and the mountains create the background for this genteel residence and its flower garden in Ohinetahi, New Zealand.

126 • A small formal garden in Christchurch, New Zealand.

127 • The mane of this stone lion in a garden in Christchurch, New Zealand, is made of ivy.

128 • Tirtagangga Garden in Bali, Indonesia, is composed of several islands surrounded by water.

129 • Numerous animal-shaped fountains, sculpted from volcanic rock, populate Tirtagangga Garden in Bali, Indonesia.

● A portico with arches creates the background for these vibrantly colored flowers inside the Amber Palace in Jaipur, India.

● Fountains and
parterres in the
Rashtrapati Bhavan
Moghul Garden
in New Delhi, India.

ORIENTAL GARDENS

The peaceful Tiger Balm Garden in Hong Kong in China.

INTRODUCTION Oriental Gardens

THE ART OF ORIENTAL GARDENS AROSE IN CHINA IN ABOUT THE 3RD CENTURY BC DURING THE QIN AND HAN DYNASTIES, BUT IT DID NOT ACHIEVE A MATURE STYLE UNTIL THE 1ST CENTURY AD. OVER THE AGES, IT WAS DESTINED TO INFLUENCE THE TRADITIONS OF MANY COUNTRIES, INCLUDING KOREA AND JAPAN, WHICH RAPIDLY DEVELOPED THEIR OWN STYLES AND CUSTOMS. THE ARCHITECTS OF THESE GARDENS WERE POETS AND PAINTERS, AGAIN EMPHASIZING THE CLOSE RELATIONSHIP BETWEEN GARDENS AND ART. THERE WERE NUMEROUS BUILDINGS INSIDE THESE SPACES, SET AMID POOLS AND PONDS WHERE WATER WAS THE SYMBOL OF TRANQUILITY, UNLIKE THE JOYFUL DANCING OF EUROPEAN JEUX D'EAU. WITH THEIR SMALL BUT WELL-ARRANGED SPACES, THESE GARDENS DID NOT ALLOW THE OBSERVER TO TAKE THEM IN AT A GLANCE. EACH SEGMENT ALLUDED TO THE NEXT, AS IF TO ENTICE VISITORS TO DISCOVER EVERY CORNER ALONG A SET

INTRODUCTION Oriental Gardens

PATH. ALTHOUGH THESE GREEN SPACES APPEARED TO BE RANDOM AND SPONTANEOUS, THEY WERE CAREFULLY PLANNED. THE LACK OF SYMMETRY IS REFERRED TO AS *SHARAWADGI*, OR "PICTURESQUE ASYMMETRY": AN ELOQUENT DEFINITION. A STONE – THE GUARDIAN STONE – RISES IN THE CENTER AND EVERYTHING APPEARS TO BE EQUIDISTANT TO IT. IT IS EFFECTIVELY A CENTRAL ISLAND WHERE, ACCORDING TO TRADITION, THOSE WHO ACHIEVE IMMORTALITY ALSO FIND HAPPINESS. THE CONCEPT IS UNCLEAR, BUT THIS IS NOT SURPRISING, AS OBSCURITY IS THE HALLMARK OF THE GARDENS OF THE FAR EAST. IN THE 6TH CENTURY JAPAN ALSO BEGAN TO DEVELOP ITS OWN IDEA OF THE GARDEN, WHICH GRADUALLY DIVERGED FROM THE CHINESE MODEL. THE *SAKUTEIKI* ("RECORDS OF GARDEN MAKING") – AN 11TH-CENTURY MANUSCRIPT THAT IS THE OLDEST TREATISE ON THE ART OF JAPANESE GARDENS – NOTES THAT ONE MUST TRY TO REPRODUCE NATURE IN

Oriental Gardens
Introduction

ITS VARIOUS ASPECTS. A PROJECT MUST REFLECT ITS CREATOR'S PERSONALITY AND MUST BE SET HARMONIOUSLY IN ITS SURROUNDINGS. BETWEEN THE 13TH AND 14TH CENTURIES, THE BUDDHIST MONK KENKO WROTE THE *TSUREZUREGUSA* ("ESSAYS IN IDLENESS"), A JAPANESE LITERARY CLASSIC. ACCORDING TO ONE OF ITS PASSAGES, "THE AUTUMN MOON IS INCOMPARABLY BEAUTIFUL. ANY MAN WHO SUPPOSES THE MOON IS ALWAYS THE SAME, REGARDLESS OF THE SEASON, AND IS THEREFORE UNABLE TO DETECT THE DIFFERENCE IN AUTUMN, MUST BE EXCEEDINGLY INSENSITIVE." LIKEWISE, THE ORIENTAL GARDEN IS NEVER THE SAME: THE MINIATURIZATION AND ABSTRACTION OF NATURE, SYNTHESIS AND SIMPLIFICATION, TRANSFORM IT INTO A PHILOSOPHICAL WORK, THE QUEST FOR ABSOLUTE FORM, A PURE AND ENCHANTED PLACE IN WHICH THE HUMAN PRESENCE IS VIEWED ALMOST AS AN INTRUSION.

A Zen garden with its typical pebbled concentric circles.

A stream crosses a Japanese garden. To the left, a typical lantern.

142-143 ● A clearing composed of a stone and moss chessboard in the Tofuku-ji Temple of Kyoto, Japan.

144-145 ● The red maple leaves contrast with the grey of the raked pebbles in the Nanzen-ji Temple of Kyoto, Japan.

146 • The blossoming of the cherry trees in the Kenroku-en Garden of Kamazawa, Japan.

147 • A shower in rose offered by the blooming cherry trees in the Inner Garden of the Heian Shrine in Kyoto, Japan.

148 ● A Zen garden with hillocks of raked pebbles in the Daitokuji-Daisen-in Temple of Kyoto, Japan.

148-149 ● A Buddhist monk rakes the stones of a Zen garden in Kyoto, Japan.

150-151 ● Maples and other essences to one side, rocks and moss to the other side with a brook running between. We are in the garden of the Taizo-in Temple in Kyoto, Japan.

151 ● The yellow and red leaves of the maples trees in fall in the Moss Temple of Kyoto, Japan.

This indoor garden is part of a residence in the Shisendo neighborhood of Kyoto, Japan.

154 • Concentric circles are laid out around a rock in a Zen garden.

155 • A small hillock of pebbles is surrounded by concentric circles in a Zen garden in Kyoto, Japan.

156 • This oval, shaped from rocks and surrounded by raked pebbles, is to be found in a contemporary Zen garden in the Ryogen-in Temple of Kyoto, Japan.

157 • This truncated cone of minuscule pebbles forms part of the Ginkakuji Zen garden in Kyoto, Japan.

A chromatic fantasy of maple leaves in fall in a Zen garden on the island of Kyushu, Japan.

160 ● A stone bridge provides a crossing to a sanctuary in Kyoto, Japan.

160-161 ● Rocks, maples, lanterns and pavilions arranged around a stream all form part of a Japanese garden in the Hijo Castle of Kyoto, Japan.

162 ● This small avenue in the Moss Garden in Kyoto, Japan, is paved in stone and marked out by circular hedges.

163 ● A corner of the Shuhery-en Garden in Kyoto, Japan.

164 • A small bridge in the garden of the Summer Palace of Beijing, China.

164-165 • The Golden Pavilion in Kyoto, Japan, is surrounded by a dense garden of maples and other essences and by several stretches of water.

166-167 • Monks before a pavilion, with its typical curved roof, in a park in Hagurosan, Japan.

167 • The approach route to a Buddhist temple in Japan.

168 ● Aerial view of the Temple of the Perfumed Hills in Beijing, China.

168-169 ● A pavilion within the parkland surrounding the Temple of the Perfumed Hills in China.

170 ● Pavilions in one of the
many gardens of Suzhou in China.

170-171 ● A carefully laid out
composition in the Chinese
Garden at Singapore.

172 • Curved roofs and circular doors of a pavilion in the Shizilim Garden of Suzhou, China.

173 • The Chinese garden is to be discovered in stages, a space that cannot be absorbed
in a quick glance, as suggested by the Zhuo Zheng Garden in Suzhou, China.

174 ● A zigzag trajectory through the Liu Garden in Suzhou, China.

175 ● A stretch of water reflects the curved roof of a pavilion standing in front of another building in the Liu Garden of Suzhou, China.

● Shanghai, China, is mostly famous for its skyscrapers but in the old center there are still picturesque areas such as the Yu Yuan Garden.

178 • Several pavilions at the heart of the Yu Tuan Garden in Shanghai, China.

179 • The zigzag routes were intended to confuse the evil spirits and make them lose their way. Here is an example in the Yu Yuan Garden in Shangai, China.

180-181 and 181 • In addition to the large central basin in the Yu Yuan Garden of Shanghai, China, there are a number of additional waterways crossed by attractive little bridges.

182-183 • Thick vegetation presses up against pavilions, pathways and other pools in the evocative Yu Yuan Garden of Shanghai, China.

184-185 ● The curved roofs are the
distinctive feature of the pavilions in all
Chinese gardens, as is this in the Yu Yuan
Garden in Shanghai, China.

185 ● A hanging walkway and
a zigzag path in the Yu Yuan Garden
of Shanghai, China.

186 ● The Tiger Balm Garden, certainly the most original to be found in Hong Kong, China, has been created on various levels.

187 ● This viewpoint with its balustrade overlooks one of the pathways of the Tiger Balm Garden in Hong Kong, China.

An aerial view of the small temple in the Tiger Balm Garden of Hong Kong, China.

190 ● Cinese gardens always favor restricted views such as this corner of the Shady Mountain Garden of Guangzhou, China, without ever offering a general overview of the layout.

191 ● Expanses of water in Chinese gardens are rarely thought of as channels for boat traffic, but are very often covered with waterlilies such as in the Shady Mountain Garden in Guangzhou, China.

In the gardens at Heyuan, China, courtyards and stretches of water following on from each other are connected by pathways and small bridges with their elegant decorated parapets.

A composition of rocks in the garden of the Huanxiu Mountain Villa at Suzhou, China.

● The leaves of the maples reveal the autumnal colors in this garden in Okochi Sauso at Arashiyamoo in Kyoto, Japan.

198 • The rock garden in the horai-san style is to be found in the Ryogen-in Gaeden of Kyoto, Japan.

199 • The garden of the Yudofuya restaurant of Ryon Ji in Kyoto, Japan.

200-201 • This typical Zen garden in Kyoto, Japan, contains rocks, hedges, lanterns, expanses of raked pebbles, all surrounded by an elegant containing wall.

202 • This rock in the center of concentric circles of raked pebbles is to be found in the Tofuku Ji Sub-Temple in Kyoto, Japan.

203 • "Clouds" of clipped vegetation, rocks and lanterns on various levels in a corner of this 14th-century garden in Kyoto, Japan.

204-205 ● This garden in the Ryokan style is located at Tsumago in the Kiso Valley, Japan.

206-207 ● This imposing contemporary composition made of tiny pebbles in various shades of grey is to be seen in the Silver Pavilion of the Ginkakuji Garden of Kyoto, Japan.

This pathway surrounded by a soft grassy carpet is typical of the Shikuoka Garden in Japan.

210 • A brief stairway links this Japanese garden to the tea house within.

211 • A small wooden temple has been placed on a pedestal in a basin in the garden of the Koryu-ji Temple in Kyoto, Japan.

● A small pavilion in the Zhuo Zheng Garden of Suzhou, China.

WATER EFFECTS

- In the gardens of Versailles, in France, a gilded Venus turns her languorous glance towards the sky whilst a powerful jet of water sprouts from a floral composition.

INTRODUCTION Water Effects

ACCORDING TO THE BOOK OF PSALMS, "WE WENT THROUGH FIRE AND THROUGH WATER; BUT THOU BROUGHTEST US OUT INTO A WEALTHY PLACE" (PSALM 66:12). WATER IS A SOURCE OF PURITY BUT ALSO ETERNAL BEATITUDE: "PRAISE HIM . . . YOU WATERS ABOVE THE HEAVENS." JUST AS THE GARDEN SYMBOLIZES THE PATH OF MAN'S ETERNAL DESIRE FOR KNOWLEDGE, WATER REPRESENTS THE "SOUL AND SPIRIT OF THE EARTH" AND THE SOURCE OF THE EMENDATION OF LIFE. IT OFFERS A VISUAL AND ACOUSTICAL PRESENCE WHOSE CHANGEABLE FORMS – JETS AND GURGLES, WATERFALLS AND WATER ORGANS – EVOKE THE DYNAMIC FORCE OF NATURE.

WATER HAS ALWAYS BEEN A FUNDAMENTAL ELEMENT FOR HUMAN LIFE, INFLUENCING THE COURSE OF HISTORY OF MANY REGIONS AND POPULATIONS. CITIES HAVE ALWAYS

INTRODUCTION Water Effects

BEEN FOUNDED NEAR SOURCES OF WATER, AND TRADE AND EXPLORATION HAVE DEPENDED ON WATERWAYS. DURING THE CLASSICAL PERIOD, FOUNTAINS WERE PUBLIC ASSETS AT THE SERVICE OF CITIZENS, AND THEY WERE GENERALLY NEAR THE AGORA. THE ROMANS CONTRIBUTED SIGNIFI-CANTLY TO THE SPREAD OF FOUNTAINS, USED TO DISTRIB-UTE WATER CHANNELED BY THE AQUEDUCTS, OF WHICH THESE PEOPLE WERE MASTER BUILDERS. IN THE PATIOS AND GARDENS OF IMPERIAL ROME, WATER GUSHED FROM PIPES CONCEALED IN MASCARONS AND STATUES MADE OF MAR-BLE AND BRONZE.

ALL THE HYDRAULIC KNOWLEDGE THAT HAD BEEN GAINED WAS LOST DURING THE MIDDLE AGES, AND ONLY WELLS AND CISTERNS REMAINED TO PROVIDE FOR ESSENTIAL NEEDS. THIS IS A FAR CRY FROM THE PLAYFUL AND DECORATIVE USE

Water Effects
Introduction

OF WATER IN THE RENAISSANCE AND MANNERIST PERIODS, WITH *CATENE D'ACQUA* (WATER CHAINS), WATERWORKS AND NYMPHAEA. THE LATTER WERE SO NAMED BECAUSE THEY EVOKED THE ANCIENT SANCTUARIES CONSECRATED TO WATER NYMPHS, I.E., THE MONUMENTAL FOUNTAINS DEVELOPED DURING THE HELLENISTIC-ROMAN PERIOD.

THEY WERE CHARACTERIZED BY AN ABSIDAL (OR RECTANGULAR) FORM, WITH WATER FLOWING FROM NOZZLES, STATUES, GROTESQUES AND OTHER ELEMENTS, DESIGNED TO EVOKE THE GROTTOES WITH NATURAL SPRINGS WHERE THESE SANCTUARIES WERE BUILT. THEY WERE THUS TRANSFORMED FROM PAGAN PLACES OF WORSHIP TO AREAS IN WHICH THE ARISTOCRATS OF THE 16TH AND 17TH CENTURIES COULD LINGER AND RELAX.

* A minimalist fountain in a contemporary Mediterranean garden.

220 • In the background, the royal palace of Louis XIV in Versailles, France, and in the close up a basin with fountain dominated by a quadriga.

220-221 • Horses and mythological creatures alternate with each other in the composition of Versailles' baroque garden's fountains, in France.

222-223 • In close-up,
golden putti adorning a fountain
at Versailles.

223 • Jets of water, gushes
and cascades characterize this
large fountain in the Gardens
of Versailles, France.

A crowd of gilded statues animates the large fountain in front of Peterhof Palace in St Petersburg, Russia.

226 ● A Samson discharges jets of water from the mouth of a lion in the fountain in front of Peterhof Palace, near St Petersburg, Russia.

227 ● The so-called Grand Cascade and the canal in Peterhof Palace's gardens, near St Petersburg, Russia.

228-229 • One of the fountains located in the gardens of the royal palace, Turin.

229 • The statues are reflected in the basin of the large fountain in the gardens of the royal palace, Turin.

230-231 ● A marble antlered figure and hounds distinguish this fountain in the gardens of the royal palace at Caserta, Italy.

231 ● The Bourbon kings of Naples commissioned this fantastic perspective in the Baroque gardens at Caserta.

232 • A fountain featuring two people playing with water.
It is located in a garden in Attica, Indiana, U.S.A.

233 • Water jets high into the air: the fountain, with its mythological figure,
is at the entrance to Villa Carlotta, Lake Como, Italy.

234 • Detail of one of the many fountains at Versailles, France.

235 • The basin and fountain form part of a rising symmetrical vista at the Villa Carlotta, Italy.

236 ● Fountains form a composition in the Cambridge Botanic Garden, Cambridge, U.K.

236-237 ● The formal parterres and fountains at Longwood Gardens, Kennett Square, Pennsylvania, U.S.A.

238 ● A large fountain stands at
the center of the semicircular
nymphaeum in Villa D'Este's
gardens in Tivoli, Italy.

238-239 ● The 'Viale delle Cento
Cannelle' in Villa D'Este's gardens
in Tivoli, a few miles away from
Rome, Italy.

Water spouts from the faces which make up this fountain at the Villa d'Este in Tivoli, Italy.

242 • This contemporary composition of a cat playing in the fountain's water is at the Glen Chantry Gardens, Ishams Chase, Essex, in the U.K.

243 • Contemporary iconography inspired this fountain, seen at the Chelsea Flower Show, London.

244 ● Masks are a recurrent theme in the Villa Manzi gardens in Italy, and also in the fountains reflecting 16th- and 17th-century mannerism.

245 ● Anthropomorphous or zoomorphic, the masks in the garden of Malvern Terrace in London, U.K., often look like grotesques.

246 • This mask, called "Green Man," is located in a private garden in London, U.K. It is signed by Camilla Shivard.

247 • A lion's head spills water in a basin bordered with blooms in Malvern Terrace, London, U.K.

248 • This Japanese garden with a charming small bridge rises on Bainbridge Island in Washington State, U.S.A.

249 • Pat Rae designed this urban garden located in the Coach House in London, U.K.

250 • Water gushes from a bamboo reed into a small basin in this London garden, U.K.

251 • A group of basins, water chains and bridges characterize a small blooming garden.

252 • The clear water cascades into
these copper bowls at London's RHS
Hampton Court Flower Show, in the U.K.

252-253 • Multicolored blooms
surround this contemporary garden from
whose center a small cascade emerges.

At the Manor House, Bledlow, Buckinghamshire, U.K., a series of brick-bordered basins carry the eye toward the focal point – the bench.

256 • In an English garden, this charming fountain spills water into a surrounding bowl, where it overflows into the encompassing basin.

256-257 • A rectangular pool and a pavilion with Venetian window-forms enhance this garden in Illnacullin, near Bantry Bay, Ireland.

The Nishat Gardens in Srinagar, Kashmir, India, with their long enfilade of pools and jets, are an excellent example of a Mughal garden.

Shah Jehan built the Shalimar Gardens in Lahore, in Pakistan's Punjab region, in 1642 as a place of relaxation for his court. They retain their restful charm.

Colorful flowerbeds border the long basins in the Shalimar Gardens.

264 ● Striking metal mushrooms spill delicate rivulets in the water garden on this English estate.

264-265 ● An elegant metal waterbird stands alongside a rock- and flower-bordered stream at Hampton Court, near London, U.K.

266 • A composition of water and flowers enhance this corner of the gardens at Hampton Court.

267 • Water and rhododendrons below and the great house above make up this fine scene in the Cowdray Park gardens, Sussex, U.K.

In Cordes-sur-Ciel, in the Tarn district of southern France, the manmade and the natural harmoniously enclose this placid pool.

270 • This graceful metal sculpture embellishes a fountain in Burton Agnes Hall, in Yorkshire, U.K.

270-271 • A reflecting pool, twin brick arches and a lion against the backdrop of a clipped hedge make a wonderful set piece in this private garden in London, U.K.

272 • A slender maiden poised to dive offsets this elegant jet-and-basin fountain in the garden at Borde's Hill, Haywards Heath, Sussex, U.K.

272-273 • The Peacock Fountain in the Jardin d'Annevoire in Belgium is one of several delightful ones on the demesne.

274 ● Given this enchanting fountain, the name "Dolphin Pond" needs no explanation. It is at Powerscourt House, County Wicklow, Ireland.

274-275 ● Powerful jets shoot up from the nozzle held by the figure in this charming ensemble in a garden in Gloucestershire, U.K.

276 • Bamboo stems through which water trickles into natural wooden bowls are a typical fountain motif in Japanese gardens.

277 • Japanese gardens are often re-created in other countries. Here we see a fine example in Portland, Oregon, U.S.A.

278-279 • Gleaming metallic spheres form a contemporary pool at the 2001 Hampton Court Flower Show, London, U.K.

279 • A contemporary aquatic composition at the 2001 Chelsea Flower Show, London, U.K., emphasizes the water flows.

280 • This tropical garden in Chelsea, London, which was designed
by Tim Jarrett, is called "100% Pure New Zealand."

281 • A group of frogs surround this basin.

282-283 ● Water jets rise from the basins and vegetation of this evocative garden at Scypen, in Devon, U.K.

• A cascade dominates the Rock Garden, a contemporary garden in Chandigarh, in northern India, created by Nek Chand.

286 • A golden globe rises over this metal fountain which feeds a small basin. The site is the garden of Silverstone Farm in North Elmham, in Norfolk, U.K.

287 • The Christie Sculpture Garden, a formal garden populated by various contemporary "inventions," occupied a corner of the 1999 Chelsea Flower Show.

288 • Various decorated glass pipes embellish a flower-bordered basin
at London's Chelsea Flower Show.

289 • Metal flowers blend with natural plants and flowers in this small basin
in a British garden.

290 • "The Garden of Reflection," seen at 2000 Chelsea Flower Show, in London, features a glass sphere in a basin within a circular pool.

291 • Charlotte Rowe is the designer of this green area in London, U.K., where colorful lights sculpt the spaces.

292 • Colorful *Calla palustris* blooms brighten this contemporary ornamental basin in a private garden in San Francisco.

292-293 • The "holes" in the water in this basin at the 2005 Chelsea Flower Show, London, drew much interest.

294 ● Walking on water is possible in this pool at Hampton Court, near London.

294-295 ● Metal, ceramics, and differently sized cobblestones are the components in this modern fountain at Scypen, in Devon, U.K.

296-297 • Reality and illusion merge in this creation seen at the Chelsea Flower Show, London. Real and artificial flowers, bass-relief waves and vegetation live together, integrating with each other.

297 • A blue-painted, steel lotus flower, sends up sprays of water, irrigating the surrounding garden.

298 ● This entirely blue fountain in the Majorelle Garden in Marrakech, Morocco, is enlivened by a pair of blue vases.

299 ● Blue and yellow dominate the Majorelle Gardens in Marrakech, Morocco.

300 • This modern copper fountain, composed by a conical basin with sprout, was seen at the Hampton Court Flower Show, near London, in the U.K.

301 • Night-time illumination makes this fountain, created for the Chelsea Flower Show, appear painted in striking yellow.

EMBROIDERED PARTERRES

- In the Château de Villandry gardens, in France, winding curves are contained by rigid geometries together with stretches of flowery meadows.

INTRODUCTION Embroidered Parterres

Renewed interest in biology, botanical novelties brought back from the new world and the debate on the relationship between man and nature were just a few of the sources of inspiration for the scenarios created by *ARS TOPIARIA*, which made it possible to sculpt green walls and scenes. Between the 16th and 17th centuries, fruit-bearing plants were banished from gardens, and geometry – the ancient "art of measuring the earth" – acquired brand-new importance and glorification, making it possible to extend to the uniform lines of the house to the exterior. A sequence of orderly spaces distributed according to various viewpoints evoked the rows of rooms in the nearby residence. The line of symmetry generally extended from the entrance to the villa, and from there to a belvedere (or a pool or sculpture), and was

INTRODUCTION Embroidered Parterres

CROSSED BY VARIOUS SECONDARY LINES. LATERALLY, SQUARE OR RECTANGULAR FLOWERBEDS WERE CREATED, BOUNDED BY LOW BOX HEDGES OR ROWS OF TREES – ALMOST ALWAYS CYPRESSES, BECAUSE OF THEIR "ARCHITECTURAL" CONNOTATION – AND, IN RARE CASES, LOW WALLS OR COLONNADES. THESE SPACES WERE REFERRED TO AS PARTERRES, WITH BOX HEDGES THAT SKETCHED OUT UNIFORM SHAPES AMID FOUNTAINS, POOLS AND GROTTOES, AND THEY WERE THE HALLMARK OF THE ITALIAN GARDEN. THE CONSTANT QUEST FOR BETTER VISTAS THEN LED TO THE CON-STRUCTION OF HILLS OR STEEP SLOPES, WHICH THUS HAD TO BE TERRACED IN ORDER TO EXTEND THE GARDEN. THIS TECHNIQUE WAS ALREADY KNOWN IN VERY ANCIENT TIMES, WHEN IT WAS DE-VELOPED SO THAT CROPS COULD BE PLANTED ON STEEP SLOPES THAT WOULD OTHERWISE LIE UNUSED. TO CONNECT THE VARIOUS LEVELS, THE MONUMENTAL STAIRCASES ALREADY USED BY

Embroidered Parterres

Introduction

BRAMANTE IN THE COURTYARD OF THE BELVEDERE WERE FUR-
THER DEVELOPED. HOWEVER, THEY WERE RAPIDLY TRANSFORMED
FROM A FUNCTIONAL ELEMENT INTO A PREDOMINANT COMPOSI-
TIONAL MOTIF, THE SOPHISTICATED BACKDROPS FOR THE LEISURE-
LY ACTIVITIES OF THE ERA. BY THE MID-1700S ITALY WAS LOSING ITS
LEADING ROLE IN THE ART OF GARDENS TO BAROQUE-ERA
FRANCE. WHEREAS THE ITALIAN GARDEN WAS BASED ON THE RE-
LATIONSHIP BETWEEN MAN AND NATURE, VIEWING MAN AS PART
OF THE UNIVERSE REPRESENTED BY THE LANDSCAPE, THE
FRENCH GARDEN EXPRESSED THE HUMAN DESIRE TO DOMINATE
NATURE. WITH THEIR SPRAWLING PARTERRES, VAUX-LE-VICOMTE
AND VERSAILLES SYMBOLIZE THIS DESIRE. HOWEVER, THEY WERE
ALSO THE PRODUCT OF THE DELUSIONS OF LOUIS XIV, THE ROI
SOLEIL, A MAN WHO THOUGHT HE COULD RULE THE WORLD.

- Colorful hedges shape a green meadow next to Chiang Kai-shek's
Mausoleum in Taipei, Taiwan.

The garden at Edzell Castle, in Perthshire, Scotland, features the motto *Dum Spiro Spero* (While I breathe I hope) in the hedges surrounding the flowerbeds.

310 • This circular parterre, with its low hedges and central basin, is a lovely feature of the gardens at Dunrobin Castle, in Sutherland, Scotland.

311 • The Jardin de la Grande, in Aix-en-Province, in France, is known for its striking boxwood geometries.

312-313 • Different colored flowers enrich the parterre of Villa Augdina's garden, one of the historic buildings of Opatija, Croatia.

314 • The formal gardens of the Château de Villandry, which is on the River Loire, France.

315 • The Château de Villandry has a formal pattern of asymmetrical flowerbeds planted with flowers of different colors.

316-317 ● An overview of the Château de Villandry's magnificent gardens, close to the River Loire, France.

318-319 ● The colors of the flowers within the boxwood-hedged beds at the Château de Villandry create brilliant effect.

320 • This garden of 17th century origin in the north of Scotland has a segmented parterre with a colorful centerpiece.

321 • This garden in Buckinghamshire, U.K., has a handsome fountain of chipped purple rock in a parterre of the same material.

322-323 ● A small comtemporary formal garden in Shropshire, U.K.

323 ● The 16th-century garden of the Villa Lante in Bagnaia, Viterbo province, Italy, is known for its elaborate volutes.

324-325 ● Boxwood hedges, irises and roses can be seen in the garden of Palazzo Cappello in Venice, Italy.

326-327 ● Flowers of different colors make up this palette at Cullen Gardens in Ottawa, Canada.

328 • Spring flowers make a carpet of color in St James's Park, London.

328-329 • A meadow of different colored tulips brighten a secluded area of St James's Park, London.

330 • Keukenhof Park, in the Netherlands, maintains a happy balance between shady groves and open, inviting flowerbeds.

331 • A brilliant array of red-and-white tulips and blue lupins flanks the centuries-old trees of Keukenhof Park.

332 • Yellow tulips and hyacinths color a meadow in a romantic park.

333 • This bloom of narcissus at the feet of a great tree was photographed in Keukenhof Gardens, in Holland.

334 ● Beds of violets are a hallmark of Cantigny Park, in Wheaton, Illinois, U.S.A.

335 ● Flowerbeds rimmed with boxwood and filled by blooms rise in the Art and Crafts Gardens at the Great Forster Hotel in Egham, Surrey, U.K.

336-337 ● Ontario, Canada, is home to this garden of multicolored tulips.

337 ● Butchard Gardens in Victoria, British Columbia, Canada puts on a brave display of spring flowers.

338-339 ● A radiant parterre of artfully planted mixed blossoms seen at the Garden Festival at Chaumont-sur-Loire.

340 ● Small floral cones heighten the garden layout at Burton House,
Wisconsin, U.S.A.

341 ● Flowers and sage plants decorate the flowerbeds at East Ruson Old Vicarage,
in Norfolk, U.K.

342-343 • The lawns of Mirabelle Gardens, in Salzburg, Austria, are broken by plantings of blue and yellow flowers.

343 • The Casino at Monte Carlo overlooks handsome lawns and beds of red and white flowers.

The Hunter Valley Garden, north of Sydney, Australia, boasts four splendid formal parterres of blossoming flowers.

346 • In the garden of the Château de Floure, near Carcassone, France, a succession of low, cropped boxwood spirals leads to a white bench.

346-347 • This small garden in Norfolk, U.K., is partly formal and partly made up of free-growing floral bushes.

● Green and blue dominate this original Baroque boxwood composition in Prague, Czech Republic.

Circles and volutes
with multicolored
plantings in the
municipal garden
of Angers, in France.

352-353 ● Here at Drummond Castle, in Perthshire, Scotland, different colored flowers highlight the beds of the parterre.

353 ● At Drummond Castle, the curves and lines of the boxwood hedges lead the eye forward.

354-355 ● Boxwood and flowering plants define the Thames Barrier Park, London.

356 and 356-357 • The extensive garden at Bryan's Ground, in Hertfordshire, U.K., is known for its gravel paths, flanked by flowers and evergreens.

358-359 ● The wild blossoms
of this English garden create
a real rainbow of colors.

359 ● The wall in Rashtrapati
Bhavan Moghul Garden, in New
Delhi, India, shelters these
multicolored flowers.

360 ● An array of bulbous plants seen at the 2002 Hampton Court Flower Show, near London, U.K.

360-361 ● This Australian garden presents a spiral of boxwood spheres.

A restful fountain and basin mark the crossing of the paved walks in the garden at Hampton Court, near London, U.K.

● The formal bare brickwork façade of Chenies Manor, Hertfordshire, U.K, forms the background to the Sunken Garden.

366 ● A corner of the Launa Slatters
Garden in Oxfordshire, U.K.

366-367 ● A path with hyacinths and
other flowers traverses this green garden,
with boxwood hedges framing a vase
on a pedestal at the end.

368 ● A detail of the geometric boxwood hedeges in the Queen's Garden in the royal residence of Het Loo, the Netherlands.

368-369 ● Another view of the complex parterre at Het Loo.

GEOMETRIC SHAPES

forms and

• Crathes Castle, in Aberdeenshire, Scotland, rises up beyond these shaped boxwoods.

INTRODUCTION Geometric Forms and Shapes

Shedges shaped into balls, pyramids, cubes, arches and even animals: topiary is an art that strives to demonstrate the skill of gardeners but, above all, human dominion over nature. Hence, nature is controlled and trained into the shapes desired by man. In gardens with examples of topiary the message is clear: this site has not been abandoned to wild nature but has been tamed by human hands.

Ars topiaria is the art of pruning evergreen plants into artificial forms such as geometric shapes, scrolls and other figures. The first elementary shapes of the humanist period, with hedges pruned to create squares, diamonds and circles that were best seen from the loggias of villas, rapidly developed into the exaggerated forms of the baroque, with the

INTRODUCTION Geometric Forms and Shapes

REPRESENTATION OF ANIMALS AND INCREASINGLY ELABO-RATE COMPOSITIONS. THE FIRST IMAGES OF TOPIARY WERE PUBLISHED IN VENICE IN 1499 IN *HYPNEROTOMACHIA POLIPHILI*, A NOVEL THAT WAS RICHLY ILLUSTRATED WITH NUMEROUS WOODCUTS OF THE HUMANISTIC GARDEN.

THESE INCLUDED PORTRAYALS OF PLANTS IN GEOMETRIC SHAPES SUCH AS BALLS, HEMISPHERES, RINGS AND OVALS. THIS ARRAY OF ODD SHAPES ULTIMATELY BECAME THE HALLMARK OF THE FORMAL GARDENS OF THE ITALIAN RENAISSANCE.

THESE SERIAL FORMS WERE REPEATED AD INFINITUM, EFFECTIVELY BECOMING A KIND OF TRADEMARK, UNTIL THE MONUMENTAL WORKS CREATED IN FRANCE ECLIPSED THE FAME OF ITALIAN GARDENERS. TAKING RATIONALITY TO EXTREMES, GREENERY WAS USED AS AN ELEMENT OF ARCHITECTURE.

Geometric Forms and Shapes

Introduction

INDEED, THIS MARKED A RETURN TO THE ORIGINS OF THIS DIS-CIPLINE, WHEN ARCHITECTURAL ORDERS INTERPRETED THE PETRIFACTION OF NATURE AND COLUMNS WERE MERELY THE REPRESENTATION OF TREE TRUNKS. FOLLOWING THIS LINE OF REASONING, GREEN TEMPLES WERE CREATED ENTIRELY OF PAINSTAKINGLY PRUNED TREES AND HEDGES WHOSE BRANCHES WERE SUSTAINED AND TRAINED ON CAREFULLY CONCEALED WOODEN AND IRON STAKES. THE TOPIA WAS SIMPLY A PAINTED PROJECT OF THE IDEAL GARDEN, USED IN THE HELLENISTIC AGE TO HELP THE OWNER AND HIS GAR-DENER CREATE A GREEN SPACE AND FURTHER EMPHASIZE ITS CLASSICAL ORIGINS.

- Boxwood, with its small evergreen leaves, is ideal for sculpting animals like the lion shown here.

This tropical fish "swims" in a garden of cypresses in Winterhaven, Florida, U.S.A.

These hedges at the Mosaïcultures Internationales of Montreal, Canada, have their fine, very green leaves trimmed in the shape of a moose.

380-381 • This fantastic example
of floral art reproduces two multicolored
birds.

381 • An topiary owl peers at the
visitors in this garden in Montreal, Canada.

A life-size topiary dinosaur at Villers-sur-Mer, Normandy, France.

The colors, along with the shapes, add to the marvel of this composition representing Roland Rat, a British television puppet character, in Bath, U.K.

386 • Various boxwood plants contribute to form this Buddha in Montreal, Canada.

387 • A seated gentleman greets visitors to the Daily Telegraph garden at the Chelsea Flower Show, U.K.

388-389 ● This whimsical topiary cow appears to be wearing a show winner's red rosette.

389 ● A detail of a plant trimmed in the shape of a moose.

● A singular gardener is at work
in Winterhaven in Florida, U.S.A.

390-391 • Pedestals add dignity to
the animals in this trimmed-hedge
in Portsmouth, Rhode Island, U.S.A.

391 • A close-up of a life-sized elephant
developed from boxwood plants.

394-395 • A dreamlike peacock in a garden in Chaumont, France.

395 • A peacock stands in front of a town hall in Pas-de-Calais department, France.

396 • Mayan iconography inspires these faces sculpted in boxwood in South America.

397 • The garden at Malmesbury Abbey, in Wiltshire, U.K., boasts this large handsome face.

398 ● A large rabbit's head camps in the Salcebo Cemetery in Ecuador.

398-399 ● An incredibly realistic face emerges from the vegetation in this garden in Montreal, Canada.

400 • This little bear in a topiary garden in Portsmouth, Rhode Island, U.S.A., appears to be greeting visitors.

401 • A splendid tortoise adds to the topiary garden in Portsmouth, Rhode Island, U.S.A.

402 ● A rearing horse at the center of a flowerbed dominates this romantic garden in Luçon, western France.

403 ● A topiary version of a St George and the dragon in Dorchester, Yorkshire, U.K.

404 • A baseball player ready to pitch in a garden in Dorchester, Yorkshire, U.K.

404-405 • An "equestrian competition" in Merano, in the Trentino Alto Adige, Italy.

● Multi-colored ducks populate a garden in Mainau, Germany.

408 • The beak was the only thing added to this topiary bird.

409 • This hanging garden is embellished by a bird in a nest made of potted plant trimmings.

410-411 ● Numerous topiary characters populate this garden in Columbus City, Ohio, U.S.A.

411 ● Two very elegant figures in a garden in Winterhaven, Florida, U.S.A.

412 • Zoomorphic boxwood shapes
stand out in the gardens of Mount
Ephraim, in Kent, U.K.

412-413 • Real and artificial birds contrast
sharply in the Villa Garzoni gardens
in Collodi, Tuscany, Italy.

A cow with calf decorates this garden in Bombay, India.

An unlikely pairing
of a locomotive with
a gondola in
Rangeworthy,
Devon, U.K.

● Curious geometrical and fantastic shapes emerge from skillfully trimmed hedges in the gardens at Leven's Hall, Cumbria, U.K.

420 • Gardener-sculptors have created striking geometric forms in the garden at Ballymalloe Cookery School, Co. Cork, Ireland.

420-421 • This suggestive composition of geometrical solids, inspired by Euclidian geometry, decorates the grounds of Wingfield College,Suffolk, U.K.

A curious room interior, complete with fireplace, at Chatsworth, in Derbyshire, U.K.

424-425 • A glimpse of the garden at Earlshall Castle, in Fife, Scotland.

425 • This boxwood-bordered parterre has carved out of a hillside in Provence, France.

Boxwood "clouds"
flank a staircase
in the Koya-Ryujin
Quasi-National Park
in Honshu, Japan.

428-429 • Ample topiary arcades welcome worshippers to St Raphael's Church in Zancero, Costa Rica.

430-431 • A large hedge-bordered in the Mary Stewart Gardens in Montecito, California, contains many varied geometrical compositions.

● A series of arches frames the stone-flagged path in the garden of Prieuré Notre Dame, in France.

434 • A boxwood crown tops an arch in the gardens at Leven's Hall, in Cumbria, U.K.

435 • The long view in the garden at Stourton House, Wiltshire, U.K., is framed by portals of trimmed cypresses.

This tree in Mendocino County in California, U.S.A., challenges the traditional mushroom.

438 ● Two spirals rise in this garden in Essex, U.K.

438-439 ● Conifers trimmed into spirals flank an avenue in the Minter Gardens in Chilliwack, British Columbia, Canada.

440-441 • Pyramids, bowls, hemispheres
and other classical elements characterize
the gardens of Leven's Hall,
in Cumbria, U.K.

441 • This garden in Cornwall, U.K.,
features a foliage cone pierced
by doorway.

Lost AMONG the GREEN

Spiral patterns add interest to the route through this maze at Longleat House, in Wiltshire, U.K.

ENOUGH TO PUT THEMSELVES TO THE TEST. THE CENTER – A COLUMN, A TREE, A BELVEDERE OR PERHAPS EVEN JUST A PLACE TO SIT – IS ALWAYS PRESENT WITH A POWERFULLY SYMBOLIC MEANING. THE MOST COMMON TYPE OF PATH IN THE EARLIEST MAZES WAS ONE IN WHICH RANDOM CHOICE AND THE IDEA OF TRYING ONE'S FORTUNE WERE PART OF A GAME THAT WAS BOTH ROMANTIC AND INTELLECTUAL, DRAWING ON THE POETICS OF THE CROSSROADS AND OF UNCERTAINTY. IN THE LATE 17TH CENTURY THE FRENCH SCHOOL DEVISED A NEW TECHNIQUE IN WHICH TREES AND HEDGES WERE PLANTED CLOSE TOGETHER, AND THEN PATHS WERE "CARVED" FROM THE TANGLE OF VEGETATION. THIS TYPE IS ALSO KNOWN AS A *BOSQUET* OR WILDERNESS. BENCHES, STATUES, FOUNTAINS AND SHRINES WOULD BE SET ALONG THE PATH TO DELIGHT THOSE WHO HAD VENTURED INTO THE MAZE. PINWHEEL MAZES INSTEAD SEEMED TO CATER TO THE FOCUS ON THE CENTER. IN THESE EXAMPLES, THE

Lost Among the Green
Introduction

CLEARING IN THE MIDDLE WAS REACHED DIRECTLY FROM THE EN-
TRANCE TO THE MAZE AND THE PATHS EXTENDING FROM IT LED TO
OTHER CLEARINGS WITH FOUNTAINS, FLOWERBEDS OR SECLUDED
GREEN "ROOMS." BOX, YEW AND MYRTLE – ALL OF WHICH ARE SLOW-
GROWING SHRUBS WITH DENSE, SMALL-LEAVED FOLIAGE – WERE
GENERALLY CHOSEN. NEVERTHELESS, IT WAS THE BAROQUE GARDEN
THAT TRULY CELEBRATED THE MAZE, WHICH WAS MERELY A WINDING
PATH THAT LED TO A DESTINATION: LITTLE DID IT MATTER IF IT INVOLVED
AN EVOCATIVE GAME, A SECLUDED LUDUS FOR A PRIVILEGED FEW OR
THE BACKDROP FOR BAROQUE MERRYMAKING. THE MAISON
DEDALUS, AS THE MAZE WAS DUBBED IN FRANCE, ENRICHED THE
COMPOSITION OF THE FINEST GARDENS FOR CENTURIES.

447 • Little bridges serve to connect sections of this large maze in Sussex, U.K.

448-449 • This striking square maze is a feature of garden at Hever Castle, in Kent, U.K.

A recently created maze at the Denver Botanic Garden, in Colorado, U.S.A.

452 • Hedges planted in curved lines dictate the overall pattern of this small, modern maze at Glendurgan Garden, in Cornwall, U.K.

453 • Though not very high, the dense hedges of the maze at Glendurgan Garden, in Cornwall, U.K., baffle visitors, compelling them to follow a circuitous route to the end-point.

454-455 • Several different entry points invite enterprising visitors to experiment before hoping to reach the center of this ancient maze below the walls of an old castle.

455 • An aerial view of the maze in the park at Rignac, in the Loire Valley, France.

456-457 ● This 17th-century maze at Villa Pisani in Stra, in the Veneto region, is one of the most famous in Italy.

457 ● High, dense, clipped hedges and an irregular route challenge visitors navigating the maze at Glendurgan Gardens near Falmouth, in Cornwall, U.K.

458 • This maze in the garden of Conholt House, near Tangley in Hampshire, U.K., has the shape of a foot.

459 • Leeds Castle, in Kent, U.K, is known for its compact maze.

460 • This maze, cleverly created using box trees, could almost be an abstract sculpture.

460-461 • A solid four-square triumphal arch serves as the entrance to this maze at Somerleyton Hall, in Suffolk, U.K.

The prize for those willing to challenge the Amazing Hedge Puzzle at Symonds Yat, in Herefordshire, U.K., is a relaxing rest in the gazebo at the maze's center.

464-465 ● The maze at Bourton House in Gloucestershire, U.K., is rigidly symmetrical with pyramids and balls trimmed from boxwood as added decorations.

465 ● A large grassy area adjoins the maze at Scholteshof, in Belgium.

466 • The maze at Structon's Heath in Worcestershire, U.K., is square and its pathways strictly geometrical.

467 • This maze in Hampshire, U.K., is circular in shape and generously proportioned.

468-469 • The Hever Castle maze, in Kent, U.K, is known for its high hedges.

470-471 • Just as with every maze deserving respect, the one at Villa Pisani at Stra, in Italy, confuses the visitor, blocking the view with stretches of dense hedge.

TIME MACHINES

An armillary sphere resting on a seahorse stands out on the green lawn surrounding Bleak House in Surrey, U.K.

INTRODUCTION Time Machines

THE FIRST TO APPEAR WERE SUN CLOCKS (SUNDIALS, ARMILLARY SPHERES AND SIMILAR DEVICES). MECHANICAL CLOCKS – WALL CLOCKS, FOLLOWED BY POCKET WATCHES AND WRISTWATCHES – ARE RATHER RECENT INVENTIONS. IN EVERY ERA, THOSE WHO POSSESSED TIME WIELDED POWER OR ENJOYED SOME ADVANTAGE. PLACING A CLOCK IN FRONT OF ONE'S RESIDENCE HAS ALWAYS REPRESENTED THE DESIRE TO CONTROL THE PASSAGE OF TIME AND APPEAR AS ONE WHO CAN DOMINATE THE COURSE OF EVENTS.

INVENTED IN THE LATE 13TH OR EARLY 14TH CENTURY, MECHANICAL CLOCKS BECAME WIDESPREAD IN THE 1700S AND WERE SET IN PEDIMENTS AND GABLES, ALTERNATING WITH COATS OF ARMS. THEIR SOPHISTICATED MECHANISMS LENT NEW VALUE TO FAÇADES BY ADDING A DYNAMIC ELEMENT THAT PERFECTLY MIRRORED THE VIBRANT GRAND SIÈCLE.

INTRODUCTION Time Machines

SUN CLOCKS CAN BE HORIZONTAL DIALS, VERTICAL DIALS OR MERIDIAN LINES WITH A PINHOLE APERTURE. THE LATTER WERE USED MAINLY IN PLACES OF WORSHIP, BUT HORIZONTAL AND VERTICAL DIALS HAVE ALWAYS BEEN BOTH FUNCTIONAL AND HIGHLY ORNAMENTAL. THE HORIZONTAL TYPE WAS UNQUES-TIONABLY ONE OF THE FIRST SUN CLOCKS AND WAS USED IN A VARIETY OF FORMS. THE SIMPLEST WAS A VERTICAL ROD THAT WAS WIDESPREAD IN EGYPT AS EARLY AS 4000 YEARS AGO AND ITS DEVELOPMENT LED TO THE CUSTOM OF ERECTING OBELISKS IN THE MIDDLE OF SQUARES.

THE EGYPTIANS SET UP MANY OF THEM FOR THIS VERY PUR-POSE. THE DIRECTION AND LENGTH OF THE SHADOW PRO-JECTED ON A PLANE INDICATED NOT ONLY THE PASSAGE OF THE HOURS BUT ALSO PROVIDED VALUABLE INFORMATION ABOUT THE SEASONS.

Time Machines

Introduction

IN 1363 GIOVANNI DE' DONDI, A PHYSICIAN, CHEMIST, MATHE-
MATICIAN AND ASTRONOMER FROM PADUA, BUILT A FAMOUS
INSTRUMENT THAT HIS CONTEMPORARIES REFERRED TO AS
AN ASTRARIUM. AS ITS NAME REVEALS, THIS ELABORATE CON-
TRAPTION REPRODUCED THE MOTION OF THE CELESTIAL BOD-
IES. THE BASE WAS AN ACTUAL CLOCK, WHEREAS THE UPPER
PART HAD A MECHANISM THAT SHOWED THE ORBITS OF THE
SUN, MOON, MARS, MERCURY, VENUS, JUPITER AND SATURN.
THUS, THE ARMILLARY SPHERE, WITH ITS AERIAL CIRCLES
POISED IN SPACE, DREW TOGETHER THE SACRED AND THE
PROFANE, SCIENCE AND POWER, TECHNOLOGY AND ART. AND,
SUSPENDED BETWEEN HEAVEN AND EARTH, IT JUXTAPOSED
THE INFINITELY SMALL (THE GARDEN) AND THE INFINITELY
LARGE (THE UNIVERSE).

- A copper sundial mounted on a pedestal against a background of maple leaves.

478 • An unusual zoomorphic sundial in Benthurst Park,
in Johannesburg, South Africa.

479 • This sophisticated sundial references the seasons, thus facilitating
accurate reading in the successive months of the year.

• Rose petals restrict
the view of this sundial,
whose pointer rests
on a dove.

At the center of this parterre at Alderney Grange, U.K., flowerbeds in full bloom surround an armillary sphere.

484 ● This gilded armillary sphere makes a bold statement in a private garden in Amsterdam, the Netherlands.

484-485 ● A small private garden in Amsterdam is home to a circular parterre with an armillary sphere at its center.

486 • This contemporary garden features a traditional armillary sphere on a stone base.

487 • A sundial marks the crossing point of two brick-paved pathways.

488 • A low cylindrical boxwood hedge surrounds the base of the armillary sphere at the center of this garden

489 • A sundial overlooks a bench in this secluded green corner.

Semi-hidden in this informal English garden, an elegant armillary sphere rises above its luxuriantly flowering surroundings.

A group of putti holds up a dish supporting a sundial against a background of white roses and other flowers in this garden in the U.K.

494 ● The garden at Holker Hall, in Cumbria, U.K., has a modern sundial in the shape of a dish.

494-495 ● A medieval armillary sphere under a pergola in a garden in Herefordshire, U.K.

• This armillary sphere that Harber David designed for the Angel Collins Garden in Northamptonshire, U.K., appears to be a piece of modern sculpture.

498 ● An elaborate armillary sphere in late Baroque style.

498-499 ● Its placement on a high pedestal ensures that this armillary sphere in the Lord Carrington Garden in Buckinghamshire, U.K., will serve as the focal point in this long perspective.

500 ● A gracious sundial painted on a wall projects an illusive effect.

501 ● This contemporary clock was included in a wall decoration framed
by vegetation in the 2007 Chelsea Flower Show, London.

502 • A contemporary metal sundial mounted on a pedestal.

503 • Half-hidden by the blooming flowers and other vegetation this armillary sphere adds charm to this private garden.

AMOR VINCIT OMNIA

Equatorial

Bentley Court

504 • A bat's wing casts the needed shadow on this lapis lazuli colored sundial.

505 • An elegant and slender base supports this sundial set against a flowering background at the 2007 Hampton Court Flower Show, near London.

GREEN HOUSES

- A dense grid in light alloy and glass hangs over a luxuriant potted vegetation inside a greenhouse.

INTRODUCTION Greenhouses

LEMON HOUSES WERE THE FIRST TO BECOME POPU-
LAR. THEY WERE SIMPLY LARGE ROOMS THAT HAD FEW DOORS,
LARGE WINDOWS AND VIRTUALLY NO DECORATION. IN THE LATE
16TH CENTURY THESE CONSTRUCTIONS BEGAN TO BE USED IN
GARDENS ACROSS EUROPE, PARTICULARLY IN ENGLAND, AND
WERE REFERRED TO AS ORANGERIES. THEY BECAME ELABO-
RATE ARCHITECTURAL WORKS IN THEIR OWN RIGHT AND WERE
OFTEN SEPARATE FROM THE MAIN RESIDENCE.

GREENHOUSES AND CONSERVATORIES DEVELOPED FROM
THESE STRUCTURES AND BECAME POPULAR IN THE 19TH CEN-
TURY. THE CRYSTAL PALACE, DESIGNED BY JOSEPH PAXTON
AND ERECTED IN 1851, MAY WELL HAVE BEEN THE MOST SPLEN-
DID PLANT CONTAINER EVER BUILT AND IT WAS A MONUMENT
TO THE ENGLISH SENSITIVITY TO NATURE TYPICAL OF THE RO-
MANTIC AND VICTORIAN PERIODS. IT WAS AN ENORMOUS

SPACE IN WHICH TO RECREATE – IN MINIATURE – A TYPE OF NA-
TURE FOREIGN TO THOSE SURROUNDINGS. ALTHOUGH NOT
ALL THE STRUCTURES IT INSPIRED WERE QUITE AS MONUMEN-
TAL, THE CRYSTAL PALACE WAS LONG A MODEL TO BE IMITAT-
ED. THESE LARGE GREENHOUSES HOUSED EXOTIC TREES,
SHRUBS AND BUSHES PLANTED ON EVERGREEN LAWNS THAT
ENCIRCLED POOLS AND PONDS: THE VERY IMAGE OF THE RO-
MANTIC GARDEN. WINTER GARDENS WERE THUS CREATED.
BETTER KNOWN BY THEIR FRENCH NAME, JARDINS D'HIVER,
THEY WERE PLACES OF STUDY AND EXPERIMENTATION, BUT
ABOVE ALL THEY WERE VENUES WHERE THE MIDDLE CLASS
COULD ENJOY A STROLL. ALTHOUGH THEY WERE SET IN
GREEN SPACES, THESE GARDENS WERE NOT ALWAYS PRIVATE.
LIKE PAXTON'S CRYSTAL PALACE, THEY COULD BE USED DUR-
ING EXPOSITIONS OR IN PUBLIC PARKS, BECOMING A TYPE OF

Greenhouses

MUSEUM WHERE ENTHUSIASTS AND EXPERTS ALIKE COULD DEVOTE THEMSELVES TO THEIR INTERESTS.

LIKEWISE, AVIARIES WERE INTRODUCED IN ROMANTIC GARDENS. INITIALLY INTENDED AS PLACES FOR CLASSIFYING KNOWLEDGE AND, ABOVE ALL, THE EXOTIC, OVER THE YEARS THESE STRUCTURES ACQUIRED A SURPRISINGLY IMPORTANT SOCIAL ROLE. IN ESSENCE, THE GARDEN IS A MICROCOSM IN WHICH HUMANS HAVE RECREATED COUNTLESS LITTLE WORLDS TO STUDY AND DISPLAY THEM, OR SIMPLY TO ENJOY THEM. IN SOME CASES THESE SYSTEMS ARE INDEPENDENT, AND IN OTHERS THEY INTERACT. IN ANY CASE, THEY ENRICH GREEN SPACE BY GIVING IT THE PERFECT AURA OF MYSTERY AND APPEAL.

- Weak sunlight illuminates a stretch of water surrounded by tropical plants in the Barbican Conservatory Garden, in London, U.K.

512 • A small and airy greenhouse in Bedfordshire, U.K.

513 • The greenhouse in the garden of Scampton Hall, in Yorkshire, U.K.

514 ● The Orchid House at Wisley,
in Surrey, U.K., is home to
numerous rare species of orchids.

514-515 ● A contemporary
greenhouse in Phoenix Park
in Nice, France.

516 • This graceful greenhouse with its glass roof is enclosed in the vegetation of Malleny House gardens, in Midlothian, Scotland.

517 • A working greenhouse framed by bougainvillea. It is in a private garden in Essex, U.K.

518 • The Palm House in the Royal Botanic Gardens in London rises from an ample grassy open space with elegant blooming flowerbeds.

519 • Flowerbeds punctuate the lawn in front of the Palm House at Belfast, in Ireland.

● A small contemporary greenhouse stands amid boxwood "sculptures," petunia blooms and other flowers, in this garden in Dublin, Ireland.

● This pavilion in Beijing Botanical Garden shelters under an evanescent cover.

524 ● Gardening tools are at the center of this greenhouse in a private garden in London, U.K.

525 ● Not an overturned studio, but the oddly-shaped supply shed of a nursery in California, U.S.A.

Two large palm-houses in the gardens of the Schönbrunn Palace outside Vienna, Austria, are painted green, almost camouflaged.

● A reproduction of
a classic statue sits
beneath the dome
of Kibble Palace
Greenhouse in the
Botanic Garden,
Glasgow, Scotland.

530-531 • The interior
of the Palm House at
Kew Gardens, London.

The SACRED and the PROFANE

- The Temple of Flora is a highlight of the famed gardens at Stourhead in Wiltshire, U.K.

INTRODUCTION The Sacred and the Profane

Many gardens owe their appeal to the archi-tectural elements that have been added over the years – or centuries – to adorn an important part of the residence or give it a more majestic appearance. These buildings or constructions were often inspired by religion, as proof to visitors of the piousness of the lady of the house. At the same time, however, a vir-tuous compendium to hedonism is evident in several gardens, which were clearly created to cater to *JOIE DE VIVRE*. Thus, the sacred and the profane often found a *MODUS VIVENDI* and mutual recognition in both western and asian settings. For example, the baroque garden celebrated amusements such as the maze and the *THÉÂTRE DE VERDURE* alongside votive shrines and prayer chapels.

INTRODUCTION The Sacred and the Profane

FAITH HAS BEEN A SOURCE OF INSPIRATION FOR GARDENS AROUND THE WORLD. IN THE ISLAMIC CULTURE, PARADISE LIES AT THE SOURCE OF FOUR RIVERS FLOWING WITH WATER, MILK, WINE AND HONEY. IT IS FILLED WITH FLOWERS, FRUIT AND BIRDS, AND ALL THAT CAN DELIGHT THE SENSES. THE CHRISTIAN PARADISE IS NOT DEFINED IN SUCH GREAT DETAIL, BUT IT TOO IS A PERFECT GREEN SPACE. REGARDLESS OF RELIGION, CULTURE OR ARTISTIC TRADITION, BRINGING ONE'S DEITIES AND ANCESTORS INTO THE HOME – AND GARDEN – HAS BEEN A RECURRENT DESIRE IN HUMAN GEOGRAPHY. THE PRESENCE OF FOREBEARS GIVES THE LIVING A SENSE OF CONTINUITY, AND IN SOME CULTURES THEY MUST BE VENERATED IN ORDER TO GAIN THEIR PROTECTION.

PLACES OF WORSHIP HAVE ALWAYS AFFORDED DIVINE PROTECTION, PROMOTED SOCIAL RELATIONS AND SYMBOLIZED

The Sacred and the Profane
Introduction

POWER. AS A RESULT, ARISTOCRATIC CHAPELS – SEPARATE BUILDINGS – WERE BUILT NEXT TO THE MAIN RESIDENCE AS THE FAMILY'S PLACE OF WORSHIP. CENOTAPHS, MONUMENTS HONORING A DEAD PERSON WHOSE REMAINS ARE BURIED ELSEWHERE, WERE OFTEN BUILT IN THE MIDDLE OF PARKS. IN SOME CASES THESE BUILDINGS CONTAINED THEIR ASHES. THE CENOTAPH IS A DISTINCTIVE FEATURE OF ORIENTAL AND, IN PARTICULAR, MUGHAL GARDENS. ONE OF THE MOST FAMOUS IS THE DAZZLING AND MAJESTIC TAJ MAHAL. IN WESTERN CULTURE, THE FUNERARY CHAPEL, ALSO BUILT IN THE GARDENS OF AN ARISTOCRATIC RESIDENCE, PLAYED THE SAME ROLE AS THE CENOTAPH.

● Castleton Glebe Garden, in Gloucestershire, U.K, is proud of its Chinese-style gazebo.

538 • This unique gazebo surmounted by two identical smaller scale ones is a noted feature of the Harlow Carr Gardens in Harrogate, in Yorkshire, U.K.

539 • The maple trees' red foliage frames this small, colorful building in Biddulph Grange Garden, in Staffordshire, U.K.

540 • A small red bridge leads to the little temple at the center of Koya-san
Garden in Kansai, Japan.

541 • A small wooden Shinto temple stands amid the bushes and trees
in Tatton Park in Cheshire, U.K.

542 ● A white Gothic-style ornamental temple enhances the greensward
in Painshill Park, in Surrey, U.K.

543 ● This small Doric temple next to a pool with blooming irises serves
as a tea house in Barnsley House Gardens, in Gloucestershire, U.K.

544 • A gazebo with a curved roof stands in the flowering garden of a country manor in Netherbury, Dorset, U.K.

545 • Blooming jacarandas frame this charming stone building in a romantic park in Johannesburg, South Africa.

● The domed Temple of Love stands within a grove in the gardens of the palace of Versailles, France.

• The Chinese House was built between 1754 and 1764 in the gardens of Sans Souci Palace in Potsdam, Germany.

OPEN Air
MUSEUM

- Rising from a bed of flowering narcissi in a clearing in an English park is this delightful sculpture of a young girl with her basket of flowers.

INTRODUCTION Open-Air Museum

ART IS A FORM OF VISUAL COMMUNICATION AND BEAUTY A JUDGMENT OF TASTE: IT IS THUS EXTREMELY PERSONAL AND HARD TO GAUGE ACCORDING TO A COMMON STANDARD. HOWEVER, GARDEN ARCHITECTURE RECONCILES THE TWO, BECAUSE IT IS AN EXPRESSION OF HUMAN CREATIVITY THAT HAS SPANNED HISTORY, REGARDLESS OF POLITICAL, CULTURAL AND RELIGIOUS DIVISIONS.

THE INTRODUCTION OF ANCIENT STATUARY IN GARDENS PARALLELED THE SPREAD OF ANTIQUARIAN TASTES AND COLLECTING ENCOURAGED DURING THE HUMANISM. THE EGYPTIANS DECORATED GARDENS WITH THE IMAGES OF DEITIES AND SPHINXES, THE GREEKS WITH THOSE OF THEIR GODS AND THE ROMANS WITH THOSE OF THEIR EMPERORS. HOWEVER, ALL THREE CULTURES MADE SURE THAT THE ARRANGEMENT WAS PART OF A COHESIVE CELEBRATORY PROJECT.

INTRODUCTION Open-Air Museum

MARBLE STATUES BECAME AN IMPORTANT ELEMENT FOR AR-CHITECTURE AND GARDENS ALIKE STARTING IN THE 16TH CEN-TURY. THE CONTEMPORARY SCULPTURES – MAINLY ABSTRACT WORKS – NOW FOUND IN SEVERAL MODERN AND ANCIENT GAR-DENS MUST ALSO BE MENTIONED. THESE SPACES ARE ESSEN-TIALLY OPEN-AIR MUSEUMS IN WHICH THE ARTISTS DESIGN AND INSTALL THEIR WORKS. THIS TYPE OF ARTWORK IS THUS SITE-SPECIFIC, AS IT IS IRREVOCABLY TIED TO THE LANDSCAPE AND SURROUNDING ENVIRONMENT.

THE ENGLISH LANDSCAPE ARCHITECTS OF THE ROMANTIC PERIOD DREAMED OF UNITING THE GARDENS OF ALL TIMES AND ALL PLACES IN A SINGLE PROJECT. AS A RESULT, THEY MIN-GLED CHINESE TEAHOUSES, GREEK AND ROMAN RUINS, OBELI-SKS AND PYRAMIDS, VASES, URNS, SPHERES AND CENOTAPHS. THIS MARKED THE TRIUMPH OF ECLECTICISM, ENCYCLOPEDIC

Open-Air Museum
Introduction

FURNISHINGS, AND SOPHISTICATED AND REFINED ALLUSIONS. RENAISSANCE GARDENS WERE A PRIMARY SOURCE OF INSPIRATION. SPHERES MADE OF MARBLE, STONE, PLASTERED BRICKS OR WOOD WERE OFTEN FOUND IN THESE GARDENS, CROWNING OBELISKS, ENCLOSURE WALLS, PEDESTALS, COLUMNS OR BALUSTRADES. THE OBELISK, A MONOLITHIC EGYPTIAN MONUMENT SHAPED LIKE A TRUNCATED PYRAMID, WOULD BE SURMOUNTED BY A TAPERED PEAK OR BALL. ORIGINALLY A SOLAR SYMBOL, IT WAS VENERATED BY THE EGYPTIANS. OBELISKS CAME INTO VOGUE AGAIN WITH HUMANISM AND THE REDISCOVERY OF CLASSICAL ART, AND THEY APPEARED IN CITIES, ABOVE ALL IN PAPAL ROME AND ITS GARDENS.

- This sphere, designed by Angel Collins, and composed of various materials stands in a garden in Northamptonshire, U.K.

556 ● An unusual iron sculpture in the form of a watering can in Chelsea, near London, U.K.

557 ● This sculpture, placed among white tulips, is entitled "Nun Reading."
It is in a garden, in the U.K.

558 • This reflecting metal disk marks the vanishing point of this path. The composition, by Angel Collins, is located in Northamptonshire, U.K.

559 • A massive thumb emerges from a field in the sculpture garden of the Galerie Beaubourg in Vence, France.

560 • A farmer, created from several pieces of pottery, is half-hidden among the vegetation in the garden of Whichford Pottery, in Warwickshire, U.K.

561 • This sculpture by Anthony Rogers, entitled "Feast," is situated in a field on the edge of a brook, in the U.K.

562 • Encircled by tulips, this contemporary sculpture by Ellen Sinclair stands in Pashley
Manor Gardens in East Sussex, U.K.

563 • This female head by Clive Nichols graces the Chicago Botanic Garden.

564 • This sculpture of a boy seated on a rock is located in the John Massey Garden in Worcestershire, in the U.K.

565 • Another sculpture of a seated boy, from Denmans Garden, Fontwell, in West Sussex, in the U.K., is made of bronze and sits atop a pedestal among stones.

A statue in bronze of a young girl thinking rests on a pedestal in Tatton Park, in Cheshire, U.K., amid flowers and plants.

568 • The profile of this sculpture by Niki de Saint Phalle, at the Galerie Beaubourg in Vence, France, is outlined against the sky.

569 • A field of corn inside a park in Westonbirt, Gloucestershire, U.K., surrounds this sculpture created by Clive Nichols from an open painted cylinder.

This bronze statue of a young woman who "observes" the flowers from a pedestal in the garden of Coughton Court, near Alcester, U.K., is the work of Andrew Lawson.

572 ● Rhododendrons border this pool containing a sculpture of a crane at its center, at Holker Hall, in Cumbria, U.K.

573 ● Two sculptures of swans "swim" through the ornamental grass in this contemporary garden in Staffordshire, U.K.

● This sculpture was created for the 2006 Chelsea Flower Show, London.
The woman, whose hair is tufts of yellow-green grass and whose face is completed
with mosaic elements, stretches out in a field.

576 ● A crane in flight created from planks of varnished wood; it is in Bridewell Organic Gardens, in West Oxfordshire, U.K.

577 ● Deer, made of resin, hide in the vegetation and amid the flowers at Barton Court, in Devon, U.K., taking the observer by surprise.

● A fanciful character appears to walk down a path in this informal garden in Devon, U.K.

580 • A Buddha sits in contemplation, immersed in nature in this Dutch garden.

581 • This Buddha, situated in a garden in Hampshire, U.K., is OK represented in his traditional seated pose with crossed legs, and is placed among vines.

582 • Elfred, the garden elf,
in Herefordshire, U.K.

582-583 • A robust gardener, with rake
in hand, is readily apparent in a corner
of this garden created for the 2006
Festival des Jardins in Chaumont-sur-
Loire, France.

584 ● A tender embrace for this couple surrounded by ivy, located in a park in the U.K.

585 ● In this English garden, a young girl holds a pitcher from which a stream of water flows into the fountain.

586 ● This sculpture of Appennino is in the garden of the Villa Medici, at Castello, near Florence, Italy.

587 ● A thoughtful cherub, sculpted by Liz Eddison for the Chelsea Flower Show, London, observes the surrounding flowers with curiosity.

● A sleeping nymph and a Neptune are only two examples of the sculptures found within the Sacred Wood in Bomarzo, in the province of Viterbo, Italy.

A winged girl
in bronze appears
to cautiously cross
the garden at Hampton
Court, near London, U.K.

592 • A character made from stone and vegetation watches visitors of Mevagissey Park in Cornwall, U.K.

593 • A sculpted stone head, with hair and beard created from grass, appears to smile in the park at Lawhead Croft, U.K.

594 • A Buddha sits on a high pedestal in a garden in Kyoto, Japan.

594-595 • This stone Buddha, partially hidden among the greenery in Kyoto, Japan, has very fine features.

596 • The Stone Lane Gardens in Chagford, Devon, U.K. exhibit various works, including this couple on the rock path. The sculptor is Beth Slater.

597 • Two rabbits sculpted by Sophie Ryder are exhibited in the Hannah Peschar Gallery and Sculpture Garden in Surrey, U.K.

This seated figure, with its head lowered towards its knees, was created by Clive Nichols and is on display in this private garden in Oxfordshire, U.K.

● This contemporary
sculpted head on its
austere column is
in a private garden
in London.

602 • This composition of polished circular stones and a mill-wheel is by Andrew Lawson and on display in Stansted Park, in Essex, U.K.

603 • These sculptures of fruit by Peter Randall-Page are located in the grounds of Waddesdon Manor, in Buckinghamshire, U.K.

These two abstract sculptures are set in a magnificent private garden in Luxembourg.

606 ● Flowers of various colors encircle this sculpture amidst the greenness of a private garden in Oxfordshire, U.K.

607 ● A sculpture of two children in bronze rests on a pedestal amid colorful flowers in this garden in Oxfordshire, U.K.

608-609 • This abstract contemporary sculpture was created by Clive Nichols from steel, pebbles and boxwood; it is located in Westonbirt Arboretum, in Gloucestershire, U.K.

609 • This pyramidal trunk of steel, situated at the center of a circular pool, was designed by Clive Nichols and is located in Downderry, Cornwall, U.K.

610 • The theme of spheres is recurrent in the works of sculptor Clive Nichols.

611 • This blue stairway with colored balls was created by Clive Nichols for the 2001 Chelsea Flower Show, London. The largest sphere is reminiscent of the Earth seen from space.

612 • A statue of a classical female figure among white roses was created for the 1999 Chelsea Flower Show, in London, U.K.

613 • A composition of three fish, by sculptor Clive Nichols, dominates this pool in the Missouri Botanical Garden, in the U.S.A.

614-615 • A stone lion seems to search the surrounding green area in this London garden.

● This statue of a young boy is in Parc Monceau, Paris, France.

618 • This statue, situated at Sun House Cottage, U.K., depicts
a girl with a bouquet of flowers who is surrounded by Blairii roses.

619 • his young woman languidly observes the flowers
in a garden in the U.K.

A stone statue in the Asian style stands out among the white roses of this private garden in London, U.K.

622 ● A small cascade tumbles behind this female figure, who holds a pitcher from which water pours. The statue is in a garden in Staffordshire, U.K.

623 ● The gentle profile of this terracotta sculpture, located in a French garden, is brushed by the ivy that surrounds it.

624 • A classically inspired sculpture is lost in the thick vegetation of this green space in Suffolk, U.K.

624-625 • A pergola covered with roses highlights a few sculptures resting on pedestals in the informal garden of Houghton Hall, in Norfolk, U.K.

626 • Bare autumn branches lightly screen this admirable marble sculpture.

627 • The great pool in Boboli Gardens in Florence, Italy, has a composition by Clive Nichols at its center.

628 • A bust of Pan stands out at the end of this trail immersed
in green in Hampshire, U.K.

629 • A boy pours water from a jug into a small pool in Merriment Gardens,
at Hurst Green, Sussex, U.K.

• Two elephants confront one another in this orientalized garden at Sezincote, in Gloucestershire, U.K.

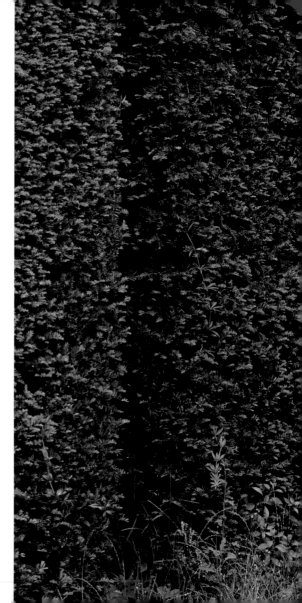

632 • This terracotta female figure embellishes the garden of Villa Garzoni, in Italy.

632-633 • Outdoor theaters became popular in the 17th century, and often contained terracotta figurines such as this one in an Italian garden.

634 • This female face, framed by ivy and ferns, emerges from the greenery of this English park.

635 • A few faces in terracotta emerge from the leaves as though they are floating on water.

DESIGNER FURNISHINGS

● This simple pergola with stone columns is the work of Anthony Paul Design;
it is in the garden of Belmont House, in Kent, U.K.

INTRODUCTION Designer Furnishings

THE GARDEN AS A SPACE OR ROOM TO FURNISH. THE GARDEN AS AN AMBIENCE TO CUSTOMIZE IN ORDER TO REFLECT ONE'S TASTE, ENHANCED BY AN ARRAY OF DIFFERENT ELEMENTS. THE GARDEN AS A PLACE OF REST AND RECREATION, CONTEMPLATION AND MEDITATION, EN- JOYMENT AND ENTERTAINMENT. EACH OF THESE FUNC- TIONS REQUIRES "FURNISHINGS" CREATED FOR THESE DIF- FERENT PURPOSES. THUS, WE FIND CHAIRS AND BENCHES, PERGOLAS, BELVEDERES, GAZEBOS, BRIDGES, LANTERNS, GATES, ENTRANCES AND MORE. SINCE EVERY GARDEN HAS REST AREAS WHERE VISITORS CAN DALLY, SEATING PLAYS A VERY IMPORTANT PRACTICAL – BUT ALSO AES- THETIC – ROLE.

VICTORIAN LANDSCAPE ARCHITECTS PAID SPECIAL ATTEN- TION TO COMFORT AND PRACTICALITY. SOME OF THE

INTRODUCTION Designer Furnishings

BENCHES OF THE ERA BOASTED ARMRESTS AND EVEN HAD WHEELS SO THAT THEY COULD EASILY BE MOVED ABOUT OR TURNED IN DIFFERENT DIRECTIONS. IRON AND CAST-IRON CHAIRS AND BENCHES WERE MUCH HEAVIER AND THUS MORE DIFFICULT TO MOVE. HOWEVER, THEY WERE DISTINGUISHED BY THE INTRICATE DECORATIVE WORK PERMITTED BY THE ART OF CASTING, WHICH LED TO THEIR LARGE-SCALE DEVELOPMENT AT REASONABLE COSTS.

TORCHES, LANTERNS, KEROSENE LAMPS, GASLIGHTS AND MODERN ELECTRIC LIGHTS HAVE ALSO SPARKED THE IMAGINATION OF GARDEN ARCHITECTS, WHO HAVE LINKED THE UTILITY OF THESE INSTRUMENTS WITH CURRENT TASTES. INDEED, *LUMINAIRES* HAVE BECOME DECORATIVE AND SPECTACULAR, AS WAS THE CASE WITH FIREWORKS, AN ART WE DISCOVERED JUST A FEW CENTURIES AGO BUT THAT THE

Designer Furnishings
Introduction

CHINESE MASTERED AS FAR BACK AS THE ERA OF MARCO POLO. REGARDLESS OF WHETHER THEY INVOLVE FENCES, GATES AND ENTRANCES, BOUNDARIES REFLECT THE HUMAN NEED TO STAKE OUT ONE'S SPACE AND GOVERN RELATIONS WITH THE OUTSIDE. THEIR THRESHOLDS MEDIATE BETWEEN PUBLIC AND PRIVATE, YET THEY ALSO PROTECT THE HOMEOWNER'S PRIVACY.

PHYSICAL OR VIRTUAL, BARRIERS ARE DESIGNED TO SEPARATE THE TWO WORLDS. ORNAMENTATION REPRESENTS THE ADDED VALUE THAT QUALIFIES THESE PARTITIONS, WHICH ARE ESSENTIAL AND IRREPLACEABLE IN AND OF THEMSELVES, YET SOMEHOW BECOME AN INSEPARABLE PART OF THE COMPOSITION.

• A contemporary garden in the U.K. with a stream, curved bridge and many colorful flowers.

This small green space, known as the Daihatsu Green Garden, is located in the Chelsea area of London, U.K.

644-645 • Rustic structures characterize this garden created for the Chelsea Flower Show, London, U.K.

645 • A wooden door at Old Court Nurseries in Colwall, Worcesteshire, U.K.

A blanket of wisteria
covers the brick wall of
a private garden on the
Isle of Wight, U.K.

648 ● Potted shrubs and a rotunda, with a fountain and various flowers, frame the entrance to this villa on Lake Como, Italy.

649 ● The access to the water in the garden of Villa Balbianello on Lake Como, Italy.

A Japanese-inspired garden in Middletown, U.S.A.

A double glass door completes a garden on Muswell Hill, London. It is designed by Earl Hyde and Susan Bennett.

654 • The "Angel's Gate" in the walled garden at Birtsmorton Court, and its walled in Worcestershire, U.K.

654-655 • This unusual gate at Hoveton hall, Norfolk, could only be called "Garden Gate with Spider"; it is the work of Inweb Design.

● An iron gate separates the manicured greenery of the gardens from the natural greenery of the woods.

658 ● A contemporary composition, with two pyramids framing a niche that contains a vase, characterizes this private garden in Norfolk, U.K.

659 ● An obelisk surmounted by a gilded sphere, located at the end of an expanse of green, is approached through a strange gate in this private garden in Norfolk, U.K.

660 • This delicate wrought iron gate forming part of the wall of a garden in East Anglia, U.K., is a small jewel.

661 • Both simple and dignified, this entrance has small habitable towers with curved copper roofs, and is located in the garden of Elton Hall, in Cambridgeshire, U.K.

662 • This portal created from sculpted volcanic rock and bricks is located in Bali, Indonesia.

663 • A Neo-Gothic wrought iron gate featuring pilasters topped with decorative elephants in the garden of Elton Hall, in Cambridgeshire, U.K.

664 • A rustic corner of a contemporary garden in London, U.K.

665 • An elaborate wrought iron structure supports a wicker basket hanging
from a branch; it is located in a private garden in Sussex, U.K.

666 • This stylized chair, distinguished by broad curls, is located in a garden in Devon, U.K.

666-667 • A stone seat, surrounded by flowers, is placed against the wall of a garden in the U.K.

668 • A resting spot created by raising the area around a tree and suspending a seat from one of its branches. It is located in a garden in the U.K., and was designed by Clare Matthews.

669 • This seat, enclosed on three sides and suspended from a tree branch, adds style to a Swedish garden.

A terracotta sofa and stone table appear amid the fragrant grass in this simple space, at Barton Court, in Berkshire, in the U.K.

672 • This wooden seat supported by a sculpted stone snail was shown at the 2005 Hampton Court Flower Show, London, U.K.

673 • Diarmuid Gavin designed this reclining chair, created from several strips of different woods, for the 2007 Chelsea Flower Show, London, U.K.

Imaginative garden seats in the form of flowers were the work of Diarmuid Gavin and Stephen Reilly for the 2007 Chelsea Flower Show, London, U.K.

676 • A small wooden bench against the wall of an English garden.

677 • A cart wheel forms the back of this wooden bench, located in a flower garden in the U.K.

678-679 • This centenarian tree, with a large cleft in the trunk, flanks a wooden bench in an English garden.

680 • A circular seat in the Chicago Botanic Garden.

681 • This semicircular wooden seat, which follows the sinuous form of a stone walkway, enhances an English garden.

• This white, ethereal
  gazebo in Park
  Cottage, in the
U.K., accommodates
a table and chairs.

A bridge, supporting a Chinese-style gazebo, crosses a stream in this informal French garden.

686-687 • This pond with a delicate Chinese-style covered bridge is in the Eliot Clarke Garden in New York State.

687 • An Oriental-style gazebo with a characteristic curved roof dominates this small lake in Suzhou, China.

688-689 • Colorful flowers embellish this Chinese garden with a gazebo and a small bridge.

690 and 691 • A small pavilion ornaments this Japanese garden immersed
in vibrant autumn colors at Cliveden House, Berkshire, U.K.

692 • A gazebo stands at the end of a path bordered by profuse flowers; it is located in Abergavenny, U.K.

693 • This small wooden tea house is located in a garden in Hampshire, in the U.K.

The small column is the focal point of this walkway surrounded by seasonal flowers in the garden of Barnsley House, in Gloucestershire, U.K.

696 • Spring flowers encircle the wooden beams of a pergola in an English garden.

696-697 • This wooden pergola, located in an English garden, is covered with red roses.

● A white bench forms the background for a pergola with white roses. It is in the garden of Mottisfont Abbey, in Hampshire, in the U.K.

700 • One of the paths in Dillon Garden in Dublin, Ireland, leads through a pergola to a statue of Diana.

700-701 • The iron pergola in this English garden leads the eye toward the statue on its pedestal.

702-703 ● A pergola with white flowers in Yorkshire, U.K.

703 ● A pergola with white roses covers a section of a walkway in this small garden in Oxfordshire, U.K.

704 ● This wooden pergola covered with vegetation forms a barrel vault, and is located in Winchester, in Hampshire, U.K.

704-705 ● White tulips and boxwood form the background for this ethereal curved pergola in the gardens of Heale House, in Wiltshire, U.K.

● Two transparent
acrylic seats designed
by Philippe Starck
distinguish a corner
of a garden in London,
illuminated by a wall
of small lights.

708 • Bright lanterns suspended from a plant illuminate a private garden in London. U.K.

709 • A boxwood vase decorated with lights and surrounded by lanterns embellishes this private garden in London, U.K.

710-711 • This wooden terrace with plants and candles is located in a garden in London; it was designed by Ann Pearce.

711 • The stone pool of this terrace located in London is crossed by a level bridge lined with lanterns.

712-713 ◆ A small metal lantern
in a garden in Kyoto, Japan.

713 ◆ Terracotta lanterns are typical
in Japanese gardens.

714 • A small bridge with a wooden floor and wicker walls crosses a stream
in a a garden in Suffolk, U.K.

715 • Walking through the Swiss Garden, in Old Warden, Bedfordshire, U.K., Kingdom,
the visitor crosses a wrought iron bridge and walks under a pergola.

A curved, Japanese-style bridge in Chiverton Park, in Cornwall, U.K.

A wooden bridge with three curved spans in a romantic garden in British Columbia, Canada.

720 ● A zigzag path created from wooden planks crosses this private garden in Gloucestershire, U.K.

721 ● A wooden walkway with a view crosses this Japanese garden in Oregon, U.S.A.

722 • This unusual wooden bridge in the Desert Wash Garden, in Norfolk, U.K.,
has a decidedly contemporary design.

723 • Spring flowers line this elevated wooden walkway in a Hampshire garden, U.K.

724 • A Chinese bridge is reflected in the water that it crosses in the Jardins de Quatre-Vents, in Québec, Canada.

724-725 • A red Japanese-style bridge stands in front of a tea house in the garden of Heale House, in Wiltshire, U.K.

726 • This flat, linear bridge connects two sections of Huntington Botanical Gardens, in Los Angeles, U.S.A.

727 • The curved bridge highlights the Japanese Garden in Huntington Botanical Gardens in Los Angeles, U.S.A.

■ VALERIA MANFERTO DE FABIANIS

She is the editor of the series. Valeria Manferto De Fabianis was born in Vercelli, Italy and studied arts at the Università Cattolica del Sacro Cuore in Milan, graduating with a degree in philosophy.
She is an enthusiastic traveler and nature lover. She has collaborated on the production of television documentaries and articles for the most prestigious Italian specialty magazines and has also written many photography books.
She co-founded Edizioni White Star in 1984 with Marcello Bertinetti and is the editorial director.

■ OVIDIO GUAITA

Journalist and photographer, he has taught digital photography at the Academy of Fine Arts in Florence. He has published more than 30 photographic books about villas and gardens around the world, and wrote *Flowers* for White Star. He has had various solo photography exhibits, two of which in the Islamic Arts Museum Malaysia of Kuala Lumpur. He is president of the Tuscan delegation of the CIGV (International World Travelers Club), and since 2006 has been editor of the web magazine *Resorts*.

PHOTO CREDITS

PHOTO CREDITS

PHOTO CREDITS

Pages 594-595 Elke Borkowski/Gap Photos/ Van Kasteel
Page 596 Andrew Lawson/Van Kasteel
Page 597 and 598-599 Clive Nichols/Van Kasteel
Pages 600-601 Marianne Majerus/Van Kasteel
Page 602 Andrew Lawson/Van Kasteel
Page 603, 604-605 and 605 Marianne Majerus/Van Kasteel
Page 606 and 607 Andrew Lawson/Van Kasteel
Pages 608-609, 609, 610 and 611 Clive Nichols/ Van Kasteel
Page 612 Steven Wooster/GPL/Photolibrary Group
Page 613 Clive Nichols/Van Kasteel
Pages 614-615 Marianne Majerus/Van Kasteel
Pages 616-617 HachettePhotos/Contrasto
Page 618, 619 and 620-621 Marianne Majerus/ Van Kasteel
Page 622 Ron Evans/GPL/Photolibrary Group
Page 623 Thomas Dupaigne/Grandeur Nature/Hoa-Qui/HachettePhotos/ Contrasto
Page 624 Marianne Majerus/Van Kasteel
Pages 624-625 Neil Holmes/Gap Photos/Van Kasteel
Page 626 Marcello Bertinetti/Archivio White Star
Page 627 Clive Nichols/Van Kasteel
Page 628 Marianne Majerus/Van Kasteel
Page 629 David Dixon/GPL/Photolibrary Group
Pages 630-631 Mark Bolton/ GardenWorldImages
Pages 632 and 632-633 Gary Rogers/Garden Collection/SIS Images
Page 634 Suzie Gibbons/GPL/SIS Images
Page 635 Sklar Evan/GPL/Photolibrary Group
Page 637 Steven Wooster/GPL/SIS Images
Page 641 Jean Claude Hurni/GPL/SIS Images
Pages 642-643 Mark Bolton/Corbis
Pages 644-645 and 645 Jonathan Buckley/ Garden Collection/SIS Images

Pages 646-647 S & O/Gap Photos/Van Kasteel
Page 648 Ellen Rooney/GPL/Photolibrary Group
Page 649 Clive Nichols/Van Kasteel
Pages 650-651 John Glover/Gap Photos/Van Kasteel
Pages 652-653 Marianne Majerus/Van Kasteel
Page 654 Clive Nichols/Van Kasteel
Pages 654-655 Neil Holmes/Gap Photos/Van Kasteel
Pages 656-657 Peter Savage/GPL/ Photolibrary Group
Page 658, 659, 660 and 661 Marianne Majerus/Van Kasteel
Page 662 Ovidio Guaita
Page 663 and 664 Marianne Majerus/Van Kasteel
Page 665 Leigh Clapp/Gap Photos/Van Kasteel
Page 666 Andrew Lawson/Van Kasteel
Pages 666-667 Christopher Fairweather/ GPL/SIS Images
Page 668 and 669 Clive Nichols/Van Kasteel
Pages 670-671 Marianne Majerus/Van Kasteel
Page 672 Torie Chugg/Garden Collection/SIS Images
Page 673 Marianne Majerus/Van Kasteel
Pages 674-675 Pernilla Bergdahl/GPL/SIS Images
Page 676 John Ferro Simms/GPL/SIS Images
Page 677 Nicola Stocken Tomkins/Garden Collection/SIS Images
Pages 678-679 Jean Claude Hurni/GPL/SIS Images
Page 680 Clive Nichols/Van Kasteel
Page 681 Nicola Stocken Tomkins/Garden Collection/SIS Images
Pages 682-683 John Glover/Gap Photos/Van Kasteel
Pages 684-685 Michele Lamontagne/GPL/SIS Images

Pages 686-687 Fernando Bengoechea/ Beateworks/Corbis
Page 687 ChinaFotoPress
Pages 688-689 Clive Nichols/Van Kasteel
Page 690 and 691 JS Sira/Gap Photos/Van Kasteel
Page 692 Andrew Lawson/Van Kasteel
Page 693 Clive Nichols/Van Kasteel
Pages 694-695 Clive Nichols/GPL/Photolibrary Group
Page 696 Howard Rice/GPL/SIS Images
Pages 696-697 Mark Bolton/GPL/SIS Images
Pages 698-699 Ellen Rooney/GPL/SIS Images
Page 700 Andrew Lawson/Van Kasteel
Pages 700-701 Mark Bolton/GPL/SIS Images
Pages 702-703 Howard Rice/GPL/SIS Images
Page 703 Andrew Lawson/Van Kasteel
Page 704 Clay Perry/GPL/SIS Images
Pages 704-705 Carole Drake/GPL/SIS Images
Pages 706-707, 708, 709, 710-711 and 711 Marianne Majerus/Van Kasteel
Pages 712-713 Arcaid/Corbis
Page 713 Clive Nichols/Van Kasteel
Page 714 Suzie Gibbons//Gap Photos/Van Kasteel
Page 715 Anne Hyde/GPL/SIS Images
Pages 716-717 Derek Harris/Garden Collection/SIS Images
Pages 718-719 Mike Dobel/Masterflie/Sie
Page 720 Marianne Majerus/Van Kasteel
Page 721 Craig Tuttle/Corbis
Page 722 Marianne Majerus/Van Kasteel
Page 723 Jonathan Buckley/Garden Colllection/SIS Images
Pag. 724 and 724-725 Andrew Lawson/Van Kasteel
Pag. 726 and 727 Clive Nichols/Van Kasteel
Pag. 736 Giulio Veggi/Archivio White Star
Cover: Franco Barbagallo/ Archivio White Star
Back cover: Clive Nichols/GPL/ Photolibrary Group

Statues in a boxwood setting enhance the Villa Giusti garden in Verona, Italy.

Cover • The striking parterre of the Villandry Castle in the Loire Valley, France.

Back cover • A small pathway in the Barnsley House Gardens in the U.K.